ETHICS FOR THE YOUNG MIND

ETHICS FOR THE YOUNG MIND

A GUIDE FOR TEACHERS AND PARENTS OF CHILDREN BECOMING ADOLESCENTS

Jerome S. Allender and Donna Sclarow Allender

Paradigm Publishers
Boulder • London

Copyright © 2014 by Paradigm Publishers

Published in the United States by Paradigm Publishers, 5589 Arapahoe Avenue, Boulder, CO 80303 USA.

Paradigm Publishers is the trade name of Birkenkamp & Company, LLC, Dean Birkenkamp, President and Publisher.

Library of Congress Cataloging-in-Publication Data for this title is available from the Library of Congress.

ISBN 978-1-61205-683-8 (pbk. : alk. paper)
ISBN 978-1-61205-684-5 (consumer ebook)

Printed and bound in the United States of America on acid-free paper that meets the standards of the American National Standard for Permanence of Paper for Printed Library Materials.

Designed and Typeset by Straight Creek Bookmakers.

18 17 16 15 14   1 2 3 4 5

For Simone, Rachel, Eric, and Dylan

CONTENTS

PREFACE

We have written *Ethics for the Young Mind* to assist teachers in their endeavors to educate young people in how to behave ethically. We came to the writing from our own experience with needing to educate two groups of junior high students. And this need grew out of an outbreak of bullying in the school where we have been involved for over forty years.

The long version of the story comes out in the chapters ahead. For now, it suffices to say that Donna was a founder of the Project Learn School in Philadelphia, Jerry contributed to its theoretical foundations, our two children were educated there, and now, long after our central, daily involvement, we have returned to help out in many ways because our grandson attends. The outbreak of bullying came as a shock to us. In short, as a result of our work, with the important help of teachers, parents, and others, we succeeded in revitalizing the ethical milieu that we had come to expect up until then through all these forty years.

On a continuum, the book has several potential functions for teachers and administrators concerned about the ethical milieu of their whole school or one teacher's classroom. It can be used as a handbook that lays out a curriculum for planning and teaching a course that will take a semester or two. We have included a theoretical overview of ethical theory tailored to the needs and interests of children, particularly junior high school students. We have also covered practical topics, providing questions and answers regarding ethical concepts and guidelines for how to teach the concepts and explore the practical problems embedded in the questions and answers.

On the other end of the continuum, the book can serve as a guide for discussing ethics and thinking about how to create one's own plan of action. Any of the references we employ to support our discussion might be useful for building the knowledge needed to understand the concept of ethics. The topics we present—bullying, community ethics, work ethic, and global concerns—can be replaced with another set that best meets the needs of the teacher offering the course. Our teaching style suits us; learning ethics is not limited to specific kinds of teaching. However, we recommend using some creativity to address the problems that emerge in teaching and learning this area of knowledge.

Other places on the continuum may better serve not only teachers but also parents and others who want to be helpful. Any adult responsible for bringing young people into this difficult arena of learning—and behaving—can get involved. There is no requirement that ethics be taught inside a classroom. On a pleasant day in the park, young people with a few adults could sit on the grass and talk between playing games with rules to reflect on before or afterward. Anytime or anywhere an adult—or child for that matter—assumes the role of teacher, valuable learning can take place. Of course, the home is the natural setting for establishing a deep sense of ethics. If it always served as such, the job of school would be mostly academic. All in all, *Ethics for the Young Mind* has a wide range of potential.

We offer many books and other materials to choose from, as well as examples and activities designed to engage young people in an intriguing process of learning. More than mentioning these scholarly and practical materials, we discuss them fully enough so that readers can judge how well they dovetail with their own views of ethics. We probe educational and psychological research contained in books about moral education, character education, moral development, and child development. From philosophy and history, both ancient and modern, we explore the roots of ethical principles. And we add resources as disparate as law texts and children's literature to the mix to weave a sometimes disturbing story with a beginning, a middle, and no end.

We enhance the attention to practical application by bringing in examples from an ethics course that we taught to the junior high at the Project Learn School, which asked us to help out with the outbreak of bullying. Declining to pinpoint the bullying as a particular problem to be solved, the course addressed the larger systemic malfunction. We looked at what in the system allows bullying to happen.

With these reflections, our academic training, our long experience as teachers, and our knowledge of building curricula, we set out to see if we could make a difference. The students responded to our strong demand to stop bullying immediately in the face of a respectful "offer" of an ethics course to address this bigger picture. Mind you, the course was required, and they never stopped complaining about the time taken from their schedule. They felt cheated by the elimination of attractive elective courses, and there were unhappier consequences for the main perpetrator. Truth be told, though, this was a workable bargain.

We see the book as creating possibilities for teachers who must cope with their own contexts—schools large and small. The ten chapters of the book fall into three sections. The first, focusing on theoretical and conceptual discussions, aims to facilitate a personal understanding of the meaning of ethics when thinking about children. As teachers, we want clear definitions of right versus wrong. Rules like these are important, and with little effort, it is possible to make them clear to junior high students. Most often, they immediately understand, having already practiced these rules at an earlier age.

Four practical topics comprise the second section: bullying, community ethics, work ethic, and global concerns. The immediate cessation of bullying aside, there are dynamics to learn about and understand. Students need to participate with their teachers in the development of community ethics—as a model for their own classrooms. Without a work ethic, too little learning will take place. Students have to come close to doing what they say they will. And global concerns reveal the larger context that embraces and elucidates the four topics as a whole. There is material enough to plan lectures, guide discussions, and design experiential activities.

The third and last section of the book challenges teachers to create ethical classrooms. To do this, they need to expand their personal commitment to ethics as it relates to the practice of teaching. One atypical practice is to ask older children to teach younger children. Teaching ethics becomes a way of learning ethics, just as for the grown-ups. We closed the course, and we do this book, with an ethics exhibit, which the junior high mounted at two local coffeehouses. Their work was presented with the help of art teachers and other community members interested in the project. Here we show the photographs taken to document their work.

A "workable bargain" is the foundation of any ethical community. In life, we are always accommodating differences. We must expect to manage with imperfect agreements. Ethics begins with a commitment to finding practical solutions to intractable problems. This premise begins an inquiry into the meaning of ethics.

ACKNOWLEDGMENTS

Above all, we want to thank the Project Learn School junior high students who were willing to engage in the study of ethics. Special thanks to Mia Clarke for the day she interrupted complaints with "we are learning what we need to learn and what we want to learn."

We appreciate all the teachers who helped out throughout the year. Noteworthy were Lisa Pack, who knows that bullying must be addressed immediately with intense discussion; Liz Ben-Yaacov, who knew to ask for help; Liam Gallagher, who insisted we pay attention to work ethic; Lucy Miller, who brought her expertise to guiding older students in teaching the younger ones; and Joan Fox, who, in her work with the children, brings a sense of global concern to our community.

All the parents did some share of the work in insisting that their children did their homework. Susan Deutsch applied her knowledge of learning through movement to conflict resolution, and Debbie Lerman documented our efforts with expert photography.

Members of the Mt. Airy community pitched in. We are particularly grateful to Meg Hagele, owner of the High Point Cafe, who offered to hang an Ethics Exhibit at the end of the school year, and Beth Mead, who guided the students in preparing the exhibit. Thanks to Alyson Silverman, who searched children's literature for ethical issues.

Marvin Hite, a member of Jerry's multicultural men's group, now in its third decade, added his expertise as a retired social worker in the Philadelphia Prisons to our lessons on Community Ethics—bringing with him five home school students whom he tutored.

From the beginning to the end, we thank our two intellectual and spiritual advisors, Ralph Moore and Frank Griswold. Ralph is a retired Episcopal priest and our son-in-law Eric's father. Over a lunch with Jerry, the three of them talked about Ralph's then-recent experiences teaching high school students using programs created by the Institute of Global Ethics. This was the beginning. After lunch, Jerry announced that he would like to teach ethics to children someday. Six months later, his wish came true.

Frank is a retired presiding bishop and primate of the Episcopal Church. Jerry met him as part of a "locker room club" that was formed of the men who worked out at our local gym early in the morning. The club as a whole gave its support to the cost of the exhibit and then offered to buy ten books each before ink was set to paper. Talking with Frank continued over four years as a guide in the writing, with Jerry and Frank meeting regularly at the High Point Cafe.

Barry Halkin, a former student of Jerry's at Temple University and now an architectural photographer, offered to document the Ethics Exhibit. The seven photographs that appear in this book were the key illustrations, along with discussion, that interested our wise publisher, Dean Birkenkamp, to ask for this book. He encouraged us before we began writing and supported us as we journeyed through the ongoing learning that it takes to write a book.

Fran Fox and Nancy Bailey, Donna's friends/sisters, who partnered with her to create Project Learn School, were regular supporters throughout the years of writing. Their love, confidence, and deep educational knowledge were ballast during the hard parts of the writing journey.

Jerry appreciates that Donna joined the team when the teaching needed the help of a more masterful teacher. Donna appreciates the intense work Jerry did to figure out an ethics curriculum for junior high students. Most of all, we are touched by our community that joined together as teachers and learners.

SECTION ONE

MESSY ETHICS

INTRODUCTION
TO SECTION ONE

What is ethics? The question is introduced in this section, containing the first three chapters. And it will be introduced again and again throughout the book. In this beginning, we consider the question in a theoretical light, though practical concerns regularly crop up; just as in the practical chapters ahead, theory is never out of sight. It is a matter of emphasis. Here, we postulate that children learn best in an ethical environment. We will not prove this thesis; rather, it serves as a guide for all three chapters. This guide helps us to lead discussions about the meaning of ethics. The aim is for students to become comfortable with and interested in ethical conversation.

On a grown-up level, every adult has a lot of ideas about what ethics is. Some are clear; others are messy. For children, we cannot do better than to begin by thinking about the work of John Dewey, particularly *Moral Principles in Education* (1909). He argues that schools should be organized on an ethical basis—under four conditions, including "a genuine community life," "an inherent social spirit," methods permitting "the child to give out and thus serve," and a curriculum "for affording the child a consciousness of the world in which he has to play a part, and the demands he has to meet" (Dewey 1909, 44). The language is a bit archaic, but the sentiment is clear. This was Dewey's idea of progressive education, a humanistic endeavor that he clarifies in *Experience and Education* (1938).

More than a hundred years have passed, and the importance of these ideas has not diminished. In many ways, they have been adapted and incorporated piecemeal into the curricula of most schools. Few can claim to be organized on an ethical basis, but the ideas are not foreign. In *The Humanistic Teacher* (2008), we discuss their adaptation and progression in the postmodern world of education. It is entirely clear that by the 1950s, educational practices little resembled those at the turn of the twentieth century. And at the turn of the twenty-first century, we once again see major improvements over what was the norm sixty years ago.

Admittedly, the politics of education, over many years accompanied by a too prevalent disrespect for the professional teacher, clouds this greater truth. And no doubt, the norm today is certainly far from Dewey's ideal. Yet a heightening wonderment to teaching and learning in our possession regularly comes to light. We began this discussion in *The Humanistic Teacher*, and once again experiences are drawn upon from the Project Learn School in Philadelphia. We have been teaching at the school in a variety of capacities for over four decades. In this first section, we use some of these experiences to illustrate this more recent expression of Dewey's theories—in the teaching of an ethics course for junior high students.

John Wall's *Ethics in Light of Childhood* (2010) is another cogent theoretical position, noted for its recentness. This new book, published 101 years after *Moral Principles in Education*, dramatically broadens our understanding of ethics. Paradoxically, Wall is a philosopher who is not an educator. He says little about schools and teaching. We interweave his theoretical musings with our practical concerns about teaching ethics to show what makes teaching extraordinarily relevant.

Standing the philosophy of ethics on its head, Wall proposes that the essential elements of ethics in today's world are taught to us by the normative behaviors of children—beginning at the moment of birth. He identifies three behaviors that lead to the functional development of children: creativity, expanding narratives, and responsiveness to otherness. Children emerge into the world genetically programmed to interact in their new environment. Normally, a series of creative acts respond to what is happening outside the child's self. A prime example is that very soon a child must learn to breastfeed or drink from a bottle. Though the act is instinctive, there is work to do on the part of the child and the mother. Thus begins the narrative of all lives, and so it proceeds.

By definition, these are responses to otherness. It should be obvious that maintaining, nurturing, and guiding these behaviors better allow children to get what they need and want. As their narratives expand, becoming an ethical person will require learning more about connecting with others in ways that satisfy their needs and wants while attending to those of others. Attention to abilities is part of the process, as is the recognition that nothing will be perfect. What we know is that these three behaviors are the ingredients of functional ethical communities.

Curriculum Outline

A discussion featuring papers and conversation among four acclaimed ethicists—Judith Butler, Jürgen Habermas, Charles Taylor, and Cornel West (Mendieta and VanAntwerpen 2011)—undergirds the curriculum. They held forth for nearly five hours at "the historic Great Hall of New York City's Cooper Union" in the fall of 2009, bringing our thinking close enough to propose a developmental definition of ethics that fits with their more sophisticated expressions. Bottom line: by necessarily living in community, we live with problematic differences. To manage these differences, we must find common ways to meet both our needs and wants and those of others. We don't have to have perfect agreement. Beyond this, all else is in the details. Some of these details entered into the curriculum for teaching ethics to the junior high at Project Learn. Coincidentally, the course began in the fall of 2009 and meaningfully continued into the spring of 2010.

Chapter 1: We begin with a basic understanding of social contracts, including laws, rules, and agreements. Following these presentations, we introduce the need for compassion, using the tension between social contracts and the intervention of compassion to expand the meaning of ethics in theoretical and practical ways.

Chapter 2: The initial discussions lead to an exploration of the fundamental problems that throw ethical actions off a straight path. We make clear that the goal is never lost, but serious confrontation of dilemmas is required. One of the most difficult dilemmas is when right meets right. We present examples from children's literature.

Chapter 3: Arguments are made for including conversation as an integral part of the concept of ethics. It is a process that requires leadership, as well as lessons for the students to learn to guide their own discussions.

CHAPTER 1

BETWEEN LAWS AND COMPASSION

As teachers, we decided to come to terms with our own basic understanding of ethics. This chapter provides an overview that helped us organize our thinking by bringing together what the two of us know from many years of learning; what we have learned from our parents, extended family, teachers, and sometimes strangers; and what we have internalized from the books we have read and the practical experiences that have unfolded over the many years of our lives.

We don't imagine that anyone reading this chapter will end up with exactly the same overview. We offer it as a stimulus—to encourage you to organize your ideas, thoughts, and experiences. The goal is to transform this thinking into practical applications of ethics that will be useful to children and, with some effort, lead to the development of teaching strategies. The job is to be compelling to children. Before turning to the even more complicated problems of ethical knowledge and behavior that follow in later chapters, we lay out the meaning of ethics in everyday language. In our view this language best lends itself to translation, with as little confusion as possible, into lessons for preadolescent children.

Should adults admit to children the ambiguity of following the law?

Laws, rules, agreements, and compassion are all part of ethical behavior, and often combinations of them come into play at the same time. Ethical behavior requires learning how to choose and blend these viewpoints. It is messy (Coady 2008). Children particularly need opportunities for thinking about, discussing, and acting upon ethical decision making with these different viewpoints in mind (Wall 2010).

It also helps to pay attention to the specifics of the injustices they feel. In these ways, we can provide guidance for dealing with problems directly affecting children's lives (Allender and Allender 2008). This then becomes the foundation of ethical behavior now and later in life (Levingston 2009). Learning to negotiate the messiness, rather than attempting to be righteous, helps them and us to abide by our decisions.

The first time Jerry met with his ethics class, he asked the students to look at the front and back covers of their daily planner and identify which represented ethics. They hadn't noticed that the words "dream," "plan," and "achieve" decorated the back. Printed on the front in an array of colors, fonts, sizes, and shapes, horizontally and vertically, were "fairness," "honesty," "diligence," "tolerance," "courage," "dependability," "self-discipline," "pride," "patience," "respect," and "citizenship." It was like shooting fish in a barrel. It's what he calls a true question: everyone will have an answer—and, in this case, the right one. He paired the students to figure it out, and within less than two minutes they all agreed: the front cover. There was no lengthy, complex discussion, just a realization that they could easily identify what "ethics" is. This was their beginning.

Laws

The idea of a law can be both simple and complex for young people (Levingston 2009). In a similar way to how they recognize words that identify the concept of ethics, when asked, What is a law? the idea is simple. Students answer with a wide variety of personal understandings. Taken together, they can be used to initiate an intelligent discussion of the concept. Their differences and similarities support an intriguing conversation that readily leads to a workable definition for any small group of students. Furthermore, the belief that breaking a law is unethical is commonplace. The connection affirms that they already have significant ethical knowledge.

On the other hand, children of this age are also aware that adults often do not follow the law. On the verge of becoming adolescents, they are particularly intolerant of less-than-straight talk and answers. It is an age where innocence meets the possibility of cynicism; hypocritical teaching or preaching is not accepted without complaint and sometimes meets with resistance. Admitting to the inherent problems of ethics helps to deepen understanding. The notion of lawbreaking as part of the fabric of adult life adds complexity, but rather than putting students off, the conversation becomes more compelling.

Throughout the early history of the United States until the mid-nineteenth century, many citizens found laws about the keeping of slaves immoral (Tushnet 2003). Those who broke them did not find going against these laws unethical. So it was, in the mid-twentieth century, when many deemed the limited freedoms of African Americans grossly unfair. Some black students rebelled when they insisted on going to public schools that excluded Negros. Others insisted on sitting at lunch counters reserved only for whites. Children in the present moment of their lives are likely to have stories about their rights and the rights of their families and communities. Other people known to be breaking laws, and getting away with it, provide an excuse for doing the same. As adults, who among us has not broken the speed limit? Are we meaningfully less ethical compared to an individual who has not broken the speed limit, if there is such a person?

In truth, we have to stimulate children to wonder about how going against the law is sometimes justifiable. Thoughtful conversation raises questions about the validity of the gray areas of ethical thinking and

---

Text Box 1.1 Immoral Laws

Slave Law in the American South: State v. Mann in History and Literature by Mark V. Tushnet (2003)

John Mann was the accused. Thomas Ruffin was the judge, a member of the South Carolina Supreme Court. Lydia (no last name) was a slave. From the record, we know that Mann "beat her with clubs, iron chains, and other deadly weapons, time after time, burnt her, inflicted stripes over and often, with scourges, which literally excoriated her whole body; forced her out to work in inclement seasons, without being duly clad; provided for her insufficient food; exacted labor beyond her strength, and wantonly beat her because she could not comply with his requisitions" (33–34).

As bad as he felt about this brutal behavior, Judge Ruffin knew that he could not convict the master. The law provided that a master had full dominion, short of the right to kill, over a slave. Judge Ruffin understood the duty of the magistrate. A jury in a lower court had convicted Mann and imposed a fine of $5. The Supreme Court of South Carolina overruled this decision, and Judge Ruffin wrote the opinion. "The power of the master must be absolute to render the submission of the slave perfect" (1).

Lydia's injuries, Ruffin allowed, were beyond a doubt inhumane. He also admitted the questionable morality of slavery. Still, his duty was to leave these feelings out of the decision. He felt bad for a long time afterward. Luckily, many other people at the time were willing to break laws to bring about change. It was a tough call either way.

how they are or are not resolved. Of equal concern, then, is whether a teacher or parent should admit and allow for ambiguity of following the law. When we are set on providing only right answers to these complex issues, the lesson becomes a lecture instead of a discussion, which can be more engaging. As always, it is a tough call.

In the course of discussion, it is critical to raise the issue that ambiguity is not license for lawbreaking. There are consequences and the possibility of punishment. We must realize that when laws are not serving the needs of the community, children will not fully understand the difficulty of resolving these issues. No matter, both philosophically and psychologically, it is an advantage to encourage the movement of ethical thinking away from the fear of punishment toward a sense of responsibility (see Allender and Allender 2008).

Rules

Donna was sitting in the yard on the bench, just watching the kids play during lunch recess, when a disagreement broke out about some of the younger children wanting to join an ongoing game. She heard Dan's voice over a noisy argument. "Let's just settle this now, or Donna is going to make us sit down and talk, and we will lose our whole break." The yard rule is that no child can be excluded from group games during recess. The children knew the rule and, with Dan's wisdom, resolved the problem among themselves—leaving Donna in peace.

Helping children learn how to follow rules is an ongoing and challenging job—for all the adults in their lives. When, however, this entails constant reminding, insistent nagging, and unpleasant shaming, the teaching is less helpful. Although useful sometimes, this kind of teaching neither engages youngsters in thoughtful learning nor encourages the development of self-direction. It is critical to stop and take the time necessary for discussion. Chafing over the time taken away from the academic curriculum misses the point of education. There are times when children must first address ethical questions: What does a broken rule mean to them? Why is the rule not relevant to them? What would be an acceptable rule? What would be a fair rule? Piaget (1965) addressed these kinds of questions. The work begins with observation. From this vantage, it is possible to envision promoting student engagement.

John Dewey

Learning to think and behave ethically requires something other than lecturing and coercion. John Dewey (1909), more than one hundred years ago, advised that the rules set for schoolchildren primarily serve the convenience of adults, not the well-being of children. If children routinely don't follow some or many of the rules that define the educational environment, and we as the adults are surprised, shocked, or angered, the naïveté rests with us. For real success, we need to be clever, creative, and tuned in to what compels students to transform and construct dictates that work to initiate and guide their behavior—socially and academically. Thus, practice and ethics are integrated.

"Too often the teacher's concern with the moral life of pupils takes the form of alertness for failures to conform to school rules and routine"; Dewey continues, there is "a feeling on the part of the child, that the moral discipline of the school is arbitrary" (1909, 15). Students are strongly pressured to conform. Though most do, the rules chafe.

Why are children so excited when school is over? Life on the playground is quite different. Students appreciate rules for the games they play. This is how the fun happens. A deeper understanding of rules in general begins with questions: What makes some less arbitrary? Which ones promote self-direction and independence? What is the difference between rules we dislike and those that seem fair and compelling? What differentiates the rules made for different settings? This kind of thinking levels the ground between adults and children.

Think about an activity for kids that might be worthwhile for adults: Collect rules from home, school, church, synagogue, mosque, work, and play. Using the questions in the previous paragraph, evaluate each one. Discuss them. Are there categories? Is there a theory that fits the data? Might some practical conclusions affect how adults and children and children and children work together cooperatively, even when the element of competition is introduced?

Common Meaning

We do well to begin with recognizing that children follow rules. Even those who break more than most still follow many. And just as they understand laws on some level, children have knowledge from the vast experience accumulated from abiding and not abiding by rules.

This experience begins even before the ability to talk. And soon, the ability to argue about fairness permits a more energetic engagement in the process. This is where learning about the meaning of rules begins and where adults can happen upon lively discussions. In this kind of environment, more thorough learning occurs based on a wide variety of intriguing personal experiences and concerns.

It is a mistake to believe that junior high students lack the experience necessary to have meaningful discussions about rules (Allender 2001). Adults and young adults can join together, the former with a deserved surfeit of authority and the latter with an admitted surfeit of vulnerability, and strive to arrive at common understandings and common meaning. The challenge of bringing this world of meaning into awareness is to affirm children's moral agency. At the most rudimentary level, children do have the power to resist and to refuse to comply. Punishment including harsh treatment can inhibit behaviors, but it is unlikely to diminish the feeling of mistreatment. If anything, it can enhance a misdirected belief in the unlimited right to refuse.

Working with children, not against them, on the other hand, encourages acting on one's own behalf in positive ways. Young people need to feel appreciated for their good judgment and to hear that adults believe they most often know the right thing to do (Piaget 1965). Successful collaboration strengthens students' belief in their ability and power to make a difference in the course of their daily lives. This is moral agency at its best—in support of social development and learning of all kinds.

Text Box 1.2 Conflicting Rules

The Moral Judgment of the Child by Jean Piaget (1965)

In grade school, Donna wondered how she was supposed to cooperate with other children when students weren't allowed to talk with each other.

> Our study of the rules of a game led us to the conclusion that there exist two types of respect, and consequently two kinds of morality—a morality of restraint … and a morality of cooperation or of autonomy. (197)

What was going on in the mind of Donna's teachers? What kinds of goals were implied? How could the rules have been clarified so that multiple goals weren't in conflict with each other?

Agreements

The world of agreements is closer to the everyday life of children, as it is for adults. There are many levels of agreements, including those we reluctantly accept, others that make sense without fuss, some that we readily see as beneficial, and so many that all of us work out together to enrich our communal lives. This is the fabric of how children manage with adults and, no less, with other children. Paradoxically, children characteristically must acquiesce to a whole world of disagreeable "agreements" as well. Some are unpleasantly forced upon them, though most are just created as a part of the natural order of childhood. Added to this array are many ways that misunderstandings accumulate. Contexts shift, minds change, and unreasonable expectations build up to complicate matters. Altogether, agreements are at times unmade. It's the stuff that relationships are made of: sometimes the experience builds mistrust; other times, with effort and luck, it increases trust.

If these agreements and those that explicitly and implicitly secure laws and rules were totally trustworthy or simple to adjust, ethics would not be so messy. Long before the appearance of urban communities five millennia ago, human cultures survived solely through agreements (VerSteeg 2000). They aimed not only to survive but also to make life meaningful and enjoyable. What was written at this turning point in history about prehistorical life reflects that we have much in common with our ancient ancestors. The invention of writing led to the introduction of more formal ways of regulating social behavior. Laws and rules appeared and were soon etched in stone and on clay tablets.

With the continued development of mores, people learned to deal with conflicts by finding ways to pursue common human goals and achievements. They worked together with an implicit understanding of the concept of agreement—no different than is needed today. Avoiding confusion, betrayal, and failed agreements, they created the practical reality of a satisfying community.

Crafted Agreements

Carefully crafted agreements give the parties involved a sense of getting what they want. No matter the age, each person is more likely to keep these agreements. The unique role of adults is to guide young

---

Text Box 1.3 Ancient Laws

Early Mesopotamian Law by Russ VerSteeg (2000)

The most famous ancient laws were collected in the Code of Hammurabi nearly four thousand years ago. In what is now present-day Iraq, these laws developed over a period of one thousand years in the Sumerian culture established there prior to the rise of the Babylonians. The Babylonian king Hammurabi directed that these laws be assembled on a stele. Strikingly, in many ways the laws—concerning marriage and divorce, inheritance, negligence, liability, defamation,

 property, and criminal acts—resemble those of today. The large black stone, over six feet tall, on which the Code of Hammurabi was etched can now be viewed at the Louvre in Paris. Getting along with simple agreements is not easy for humans. Laws and rules are essential for living with others, as is the daily interplay of workable agreements. Rumi, the great Sufi poet of the thirteenth century, reflected this sentiment long ago:

> Out beyond right doing and wrong doing, there is a field. I'll meet you there.

A fragment of the Code of Hammurabi can be found at Ancient Mesopotamia for Kids (www.mesopotamia .mrdonn.org/hammurabi.html). The site presents the laws, legal challenges, and even games that are relevant and interesting for young people as well as adults.

Photo 1.1 A Fragment of the Code of Hammurabi

---

people's efforts in this process. The unique role for young adults stems from a life less burdened by complications. Between innocence and cynicism, the involvement of the young in the process can be especially instructive to adults. The learning has vitality. The mood is one of resistance to acquiescence. The young have an innate creativity ready for tapping.

What these youngsters don't have is ease. The challenge is for both those older and those younger to give each other the slack needed to make agreements and tend to the problems that confound them.

Ethics are created as agreements—first in ourselves and then by helping others. For children, it is new, fresh learning. As adults, we must keep on learning and relearning for the full length of our lives. The beginning is in inviting young people to take initiative in the creation of their own ethics. With these efforts, adults become better creators of their own ethics, and their students engage in learning that reflects a practical realness. Learning to make agreements of all kinds forms the foundation of an ethical mind. It is a personal process that entails both outer agreements, which balance getting what we want with the wants of others, and inner agreements to abide by the rules and laws sensible to our inner core (Allender and Allender 2008; Kegan 1994).

Compassion

The idea of compassion is not commonplace for children, even those close to becoming adolescents. Words like "caring," "concern," "fairness," and "sympathy" are familiar and can serve to begin a discussion that will lead to thinking about compassion. What evokes the concept is not the same for everyone; the exploration moves forward by its openness. In the special relationship of compassion to laws, rules, and agreements, we begin by thinking of the latter three primarily as limitations, whereas compassion encompasses feelings and actions that interpret the context in which these limitations are applied. Building on this understanding, the three kinds of social contract need to be seen more for their role in creating a social environment that has significant benefits, including measures of protected freedom and the expansion of choice. This big picture serves as a good start (Noddings 2005).

A more complex understanding can then unfold. In the big picture, compassion is a relatively uncomplicated ethical stance that feelings about how others, not only ourselves, are cared for constitute a necessary part of social life. This is easy enough to believe, hard to deny, and, of course, harder to act upon. Action may be quite demanding, and the level of success may be disappointing; still, the goal is often clear-cut. Not so clear is where the ethics of compassion become linked to the transgression of social agreements. In this case, ethics are again messy and intensified over and above the ambiguities intrinsic to the breaking of laws, rules, and everyday agreements. Significantly, how compassion is applied to the transgressor challenges the rationality of ethics. We all, adults and young people, must confront this problem. Youngsters regularly ask for a break from their peers and caretakers.

Integrated Emotion and Intellect

The ethics of compassion require an integration of emotional expression and intellectual reasoning—the basis of intuition. Intuition offers a complete response to the problems raised by understanding transgression within its unique context; intuition assures ethical judgment. Harkening back to ancient history, people whose wisdom was highly regarded made judgments. Traditionally, these judgments were based on reflections that examined misbehavior and the circumstances surrounding it. Over centuries and centuries, the notion developed that exclusive rationality enhanced good judgment. People get fixed on an absolute meaning of rules and laws without allowing for the possibility of mitigating circumstances. In our minds, children are never well served by this narrower view, which fails to address the whole of the problem at hand.

Learning compassion is greatly enhanced by experiencing it (Charney 1991; Simon 2001). Fear drives the separation of the intellect and emotions. Courage is needed to realize the creative handling of transgression. Adults worry about loss of control and the possible creation of turmoil. The same fear-driven reasoning pushes the ethics of judgment without compassion to the establishment of zero tolerance. In schools, it is better to base leadership skills and judgment on courage. With a wider lens, we can see how we all differ from each other, and the problem is better served by tailoring ethical responses that join us with the transgressor. Yes, there have to be immediate consequences for the transgression, and yes, there has to be understanding that guides the longer-range consequences. Outside worst-case scenarios, with the focus on young people, ethical actions need to be inclusive, not exclusive. Compassion requires that consequences both rectify and embrace. Doing both is intuitive behavior that appropriately responds to wrongs and at the same time teaches what is likely to be right for all.

The children's book *How to Steal a Dog* by Barbara O'Conner (2007) shares a lesson for confronting the problem of being compassionate. The story tells of a young girl who steals a dog with the idea of returning the "missing" pet for the reward that will be offered. In her encounter with the dog's owner, Carmella, she has to face feelings that interfere with her plan.

Before having students read this book, ask them to make up a story using the following cast of characters:

Georgina, the little girl who steals Willie, the dog, to make money
from the reward for her family

Toby, the younger brother, loyal but questioning Georgina's actions

Mama, who owns the car they live in and makes too little to afford
a home for them

Carmella, an older woman who lives alone and misses her dog
badly

Mookie, a drifter with three fingers and a bike with a crooked
wheel, who knows what is right

Have the children compare their imagined versions of the story and
the one written by Barbara O'Conner. How is compassion different in
each story? What feelings does Carmella's sadness evoke in Georgina?
What internal emotional conflicts does Georgina have to face?

Moral Questions in the Classroom by Katherine Simon (2001) is a
helpful guide for leading a discussion about the meaning of compassion. The book is unusual in how it elevates the importance of caring
for others and oneself as a part of ethical behavior. The meaning of
ethics includes not only rational judgments but also humanistic quali-
fications that can accompany and modify these judgments.

Pondering and doing ethics are messy, indeed, but worth the effort.
Adults and children alike have expanding narratives that express an
ethical view of life, named as such or not (Wall 2010). In the teaching
of ethics, we must help children look at their personal stories. Once
brought to the surface, they can be changed—subtracted from and
added to. With collaboration, it is possible to find and build common
elements that feed community.

Intriguing, then, is how the distinction between children and adults
softens. Children do need our support, limitations, and protection.
Yet it is not necessary to assume that adults are in all ways superior.
What we have to offer each other is nearly infinite. Not everything is
possible, but certainly much more is possible beyond the limitations
imposed by our engrained assumptions. Neither children nor any others who differ from us profit from being labeled inferior. Our stories
intertwine. We can widen our horizons by learning better how ethics
becomes the work we do to grow together. We start by giving each
other more slack—a break, as we sometimes say (O'Conner 2007).
Between laws and compassion there exists a world in which we can
all expand—a world where we learn ethics by teaching ethics.

*   *   *

Toward the end of the semester, amid complaining and grumbling once again about the addition of an ethics course to an already busy schedule, Mia, generally a quiet person, boldly stopped the group to say, "Guys, we have to admit we learned what we needed to learn and what we wanted to learn!" There was a silent pause; no one disagreed.

CHAPTER 2

RIGHT VERSUS RIGHT

The next step is to explore ethical problems that pose more stressful complications than those presented in the basic overview. As experienced teachers and reasonably successful parents (with approval from our grown children for this description), we are confident that young people will respond cooperatively to the requests and demands we make—at best, a raised eyebrow will be enough for children to back off from unruly behavior. And they can expect our respect for their needs in a mix of good humor all around.

But we also expect serious conflicts to arise that will have to be worked out. Between the children and between the children and ourselves, there are times when there is right on both sides. Laws, rules, agreements, and compassion may be insufficient to solve conflicts. In this chapter, we look at the concept of right versus right, the dilemmas that emerge from this lack of balance, and an array of examples.

In ethical terms, we can no longer be hoping for what is right. An insightful analogy likens the government of modern democracies to the management of children's education. Given the great diversity in which we all live, governments suffer this lack of balance all too often. Only by listening to the many voices, believing that each and every person likely has a valid place in the mix, is there hope for maximizing the needs and wants on many sides. There is no reason to believe that children have equal rights, but they do have rights. In our view, the struggle for authority is similar. Consider this, as the argument and examples unfold.

Dilemmas

In the gray areas of ethical inquiry, believing that both sides of a conflict are right provokes dilemmas that necessarily create confusion or, worse, staunch opposition. The standard goal of studying ethics is to help young people make simple choices between right and wrong (Levingston 2009). Knowing the difference is usually not the problem; acting on this knowledge is the difficulty. But more difficult are those situations that require arbitrating between right versus right. These are also especially instructive for learning how to act ethically, and they are as much a part of children's lives at home as in school and on the playground. To recognize that conflicting views are normal, even if problematic, is good learning, as it is potentially generative. Understanding our own and others' rights fleshes out the whole picture of the world in which we live, like it or not. What we consider ethical has to contend with this reality (Kidder 1995).

How can there be right versus right? Simply articulating the question brings ethical problems, from worldly to daily, into a clearer light. How do we come to believe something is right in the first place? Ancient wisdom is the source of ethical thinking that has led up through the millennia to the complex thinking we do today (Casson 2001; Kramer 1981). Grave matters that troubled our ancestors stimulated the wisdom. Some of it they attributed to words spoken by local gods. Later, ancient wisdom was inspired by one universal God, though different for different religions. Sometimes people trusted the thinking of their elders. There were probably others, too, who trusted their own judgment in ways practiced in our modern world. Due to this cacophony of voices, then, it is no surprise that what is right for one can differ from and often oppose another view of what is right.

The troubles deepen in the light of so many different beliefs about the source of rightness that crisscross the planet. Between countries and within communities of every size, within families and between friends, conflicts abound as if they were the only reality we have. For millions practicing different religious faiths today, the will of God principally determines life's rules. Millions more, often overlapping with the faithful, consider the primary guide to be the will of majorities, while political authoritarianism guides others.

Minorities

Contesting commonly accepted practices are the many minorities sorely dissatisfied with society's failure to meet their needs adequately. Working for the resolution of disagreements in this buzzing world of tensions profoundly complicates every aspect of human experience.

Text Box 2.1 Diversity

Sowing the Seeds of Character by Judd Levingston (2009)

In a recent study, Levingston describes three moral outlooks that he found in the young people he teaches. Among students from different schools, varied cultural backgrounds, and unique family lives, he found individuals holding traditional values, those who want to combine tradition with their own values, and those who take a more progressive stance. He labeled the most traditional as "Authentic and Assured," those who strive toward maintaining tradition while building an independent voice as "Bridging and Binding," and those aiming to free themselves from tradition as "Constructing and Considering." The diversity of adult values is already mirrored in older children long before they too become adults.

How true does this study seem?

In what ways might these outlooks cause problems in an ethics course?

What might be the advantages of categorizing children in these ways?

On page 1, Levingston asks, "Did you ask a good question today?"

Sets of questions can be collected and categorized. Children can decide whether they fit into the categories or not. To the reader, do you fit into one of the categories? Is there some other name you would give to a category that fits better? What about changes over time?

Life can be so bewildering in this complex civilization that has evolved from the end of prehistory through the long journey of documented human history till now, and the next now, and on and on. There is no small share of despair, and yet evidence of much success, even progress, can give us a sense of meaning in our lives (Davis 2004).

Young people in particular need to feel assured that they are capable of making thoughtful judgments where right versus right appears in their daily lives. And they need adult guidance—guidance that is a process of learning focused on the children's own experiences. To be sure, the work does not begin with a bewildering introduction that catalogues the breadth and prevalence of problems of right versus right that face us in adult life. To guide well, we, as the children's teachers, do need to have an understanding of this greater context. Still, there is a critical difference between the reduction of complexity essentially to triviality and the selection of aspects of ethical thinking for how they retain the intensity of personal and social confrontation meaningfully. Then learning can become a vibrant reality as a means for finding practical solutions. We must aim toward a rich engagement that leads to resolutions that are more hopeful—a process that offers potential for a lifelong usefulness.

We might wish that our elder voices, seasoned by years of learning and experience, were the last word of wisdom upon which children depended and served as the advice they followed (Kidder 2005). Just as when they confront laws, rules, and agreements, their acquiescence is hardly assured. We can't make them believe us; ethical behavior is no less a personal decision for children than it is for adults.

Self-assurance begins with elders' admitting that theirs is not the last word when it comes to ethical judgment. In this arena, there is even more room to learn from each other. It is okay to admit that we all make mistakes. In the role of teachers, we need not veer from our own beliefs. We are responsible for clarifying the consequences of what we consider misbehavior. But we still teach most effectively by encouraging young people to express their thoughts and opinions and making sure that they feel heard. If this is the case for all manners of teaching and learning, it is even more so for the development of ethical thinking. Out of this kind of discussion, we can mine the problems where rights confront each other.

Text Box 2.2 A Dilemma

How Good People Make Tough Choices by Rushworth Kidder (1995)

I looked up from my computer. A woman with decades of experience, one of the best in the business, is standing silently in front of my desk. In one hand she held a copy of her young assistant's story on blueberries. In the other hand she held a battered, tan cookbook some thirty years old. She laid each on my desk. And there, on the pages of the cookbook, was our young friend's story, printed word for word. Among the few cardinal sins of journalism, you don't plagiarize. It was a pure and simple case of right-versus-wrong temptation—and she had chosen wrong.

For me, however, it was an ethical dilemma. Two conflicting desires. Heave her out into the street. The other half of me wanted to go to her desk and say, "What on earth has come over you? You know better." Since her blueberry piece had not yet been published, we moved her to an editing slot, with the understanding that she was to do no more writing.

This story is worthy of discussion. The initial problem, deliberately masked, is that it is not ours. We adapted it from Kidder (20–22). You might say we plagiarized it. But the original story is much longer and more insightful. However, Rushworth Kidder wrote every word and most of the sentences of this "paraphrase." The text in quotation marks aside, we can ask whose work this is.

For both adults and children, there is a dilemma. How do we teach our children to use resources and gather information for writing papers without plagiarizing the material? And learn this they must.

School

We take the following summarized stories from two highly acclaimed books about dilemmas encountered in schooling children in the early thirties (Carter 1976; Kuroyanagi 1981). The stories are full of wonder.

Six-year-old Totto-chan was expelled from school because, in so many ways, she didn't do what was right. She wasn't malicious, mind you, just energetic to the extent that the teacher felt beyond frustrated with her constant disruptions. The girl's getting out of her seat to watch musicians on the street passing by the classroom window and calling her classmates to come see were the last straw. The teacher could think of no alternative but to meet with the child's mother and say that Totto-chan must leave. Luckily, her mother found an unusual school where classes were held in old passenger train cars. Also distinctive was Mr. Kobayashi, the headmaster. On the day he met Totto-chan, they sat and talked for the entire morning, until it was time for lunch.

Totto-chan: The Little Girl at the Window is a book written in 1981 by Tetsuko Kuroyanagi, a television celebrity in Japan, remembering the Tomoe School in Tokyo in the 1930s. Neither her old school nor her new one was wrong. One, however, was right for Totto-chan, and Tomoe resolved the conflict. This solution entailed no great principle; rather it was a creative way out of the box that worked for everyone involved. By today's thinking, the resolution may seem too simple, but the conflict then was heart wrenching.

Forrest Carter writes about Little Tree, his name as a young child in the 1930s. In *The Education of Little Tree*, written in 1976, he tells how after the death of both of his parents, he went to live with his Native American grandparents in an isolated mountain cabin with no school nearby. Guided by the wisdom of his Granma and Granpa, he learned reading, writing, and arithmetic, in addition to much else from their unusual lifestyle. The writing conveys the wisdom of his grandparents and how Little Tree was becoming an educated and ethical young adult.

A couple of years passed, and Little Tree was discovered by county authorities. They said the law required him to live in an orphanage and go to school. In a poignant discussion of right versus right, the family together discussed the law and decided it must be obeyed. It's a sad moment when he gets on the bus to leave with instructions written on a tag around his neck.

The pivotal experience happened when the teacher "held up a picture that showed a deer herd coming out of a spring branch. They was jumping on one another.... She asked if anybody knew what they were doing." Children talked about running from a hunter and how maybe they didn't like the water. Little Tree said they were mating. "I could tell by the bushes and trees that it was the time of year when they done their mating." He was sent to the headmaster who, outraged, proceeded to cane him for his despicable behavior. Little Tree made no sound. Infuriated even more, the headmaster continued to beat him until blood ran down his back. Soon after, Granpa came and took him home. No one came looking for Little Tree again (quotes from the original text).

Some of our students read *Totto-chan*, and others chose *Little Tree*. Discussion of the books together focused on the different characters' perceptions of what is right. As teachers we are not wishy-washy; we clearly value the Tomoe School and the ways Granpa and Granma educate young people. But students catch on that this is not the main point, particularly when we talk about Granpa's making whiskey, with Little Tree's help, in a still hidden in the woods. The discussion is less about who is right and who is wrong and more about how we have to sort out our own conflicts in the school yard and in the classroom. It is intriguing, too, to read stories, written in cuneiform on five-thousand-year-old clay tablets, telling us that caning was common in the very first schools to appear in recorded history (Kramer 1981). It seems so wrong, and yet it was deemed right for so long.

Tomoe was destroyed in World War II and now seems less a reality and more like a story. And how Carter shaped his experience clearly feels more like fiction than a memoir. Students aren't concerned. For them and many adults, both tales hint at possibilities, and the possibility of possibilities, that make for resolving dilemmas. They are compelling books for young people and adults—*Totto-chan* a best seller in Japan in the millions and *Little Tree* a book prized in America by thousands. All of us have favorite books that we might share with children becoming adolescents, and maybe they would be equally compelling—as a source of knowledge that leads young people and us closer to ethical behavior.

Rights of Children

Conflicts occur regularly when what children believe is right comes up against adult views of what needs to be happening—so much so

---

Text Box 2.3 Authority

Totto-chan by Tetsuko Kuroyanagi (1981)
The Education of Little Tree by Forrest Carter (1976)
Experience and Education by John Dewey (1938)

"Authority ... when exercised in a well-regulated household or other community group is not a manifestation of merely personal will; the parent or teacher exercises it as the representative and agent of the interests of the group as a whole" (Dewey 1938, 59).

Kinds of authority:
The teacher who expelled Totto-chan
Totto-chan's mother
Mr. Kobayashi, the headmaster at Tomoe

Little Tree's Granma
Little Tree's Granpa
County authorities
The teacher at the orphanage
The headmaster at the orphanage

Using Dewey's definition and any others you have, compare these kinds of authority. The summaries are enough to make this possible. There are more characters and lots more detail in the books that can broaden the discussion even more. Either way, dilemmas and issues of right versus right abound. How do these books reflect on your own life?

---

that children expect to find themselves in conflict with adults as a normal event. Ingrained in their minds from the beginning is how the rights of others easily trump their own. With a parallel force, there is another ingrained feeling that "I" have rights—out of which the cry of unfairness is boldly expressed. Some rights are granted, or not; others are claimed.

From Antiquity to Now

The rights that adults grant to children are, like others, granted by those who are in authority. Even before complex civilizations with big cities, complex religions, bodies of literature, and schools that taught students to be scribes, community leaders created and prescribed laws. Judging from the writings of ancient people about their own past, early on in the evolution of social mores, granted rights encompassed not only what people could and could not do but also special rights for people of different statuses and need—like nobility, commoners, slaves, widows, orphans, and the poor (Kramer 1981). As corrupt and insensitive as leaders could be, at other times, even as far back as when Sumer thrived in the third millennium BCE, they enacted reforms that resemble modern-day concerns. Today, we live in a country guided by basic rights built on the right to life, liberty, and the pursuit of happiness. In the twentieth century, we saw similar international rights granted to children by the League of Nations and the United Nations (Wall 2010).

The rights that children claim for themselves appear to be altogether different from the rights proclaimed in the world of grown-ups. Adults proudly protest the absence of freedom, equality, justice, and care for basic needs. At times, a strong belief in these rights goes so far as to fuel wars. From this viewpoint, children's claims represent insignificant wants in comparison. Their cares relate to work and play taking place in the moment. The vivid contrast reasonably supports the belief that young people are immature and unready to conceptualize claims that require serious attention.

It is true that children are immature by definition. This does not mean, however, that their beliefs about what is right are unworthy of attention (Kegan 1994). Carried too far, the concept of immaturity can be taken to mean that young people are not yet quite human (Wall 2010). Young people doubtless need to be cared for and provided with adequate structure to guide their growth. This does not excuse them, however, from abiding by the basic rules that create and support a well-functioning social community. Adults can act equally immaturely or worse when they disregard their humanity. The expectation to act responsibly is a given at any age, beyond toddlerhood, and it is unacceptable either to disregard the rights of others or to discourage claiming our own.

Children becoming adolescents are in the process of learning the skills necessary to act with maturity, and doing so requires experience and practice. They need to learn how to creatively and actively participate as members of their communities—to honor the diversity of others. No less, adolescents need to be encouraged to claim rights that are reasonable within the domain of young people. They must practice articulating their claims and build needed negotiation skills. We don't get all that we want, but finding the middle ground can provide successful results that benefit children in practical ways (see Coady 2008; also Dewey 1909, 1938).

Regularly, conflicts are resolved by threats of punishment, the use of greater power, or actual resort to physical means. This approach is never optimal, although it is sometimes necessary and appropriate. Sometimes poor compromises are made that only have the appearance of a satisfying agreement. They are a pretense of agreement designed to deny the voice of the person or persons of lesser power. They are never desirable. Other times, a sense of community offers good-enough terms for working together to satisfactorily resolve these conflicts for all. The goal is to downplay the existence of power and arrive at agreements without compromising anyone's integrity (Allender 2001; Allender and Allender 2008).

In *Messy Morality* (2008), C. A. J. Coady devotes a chapter to documenting the universality of the belief that lying is morally wrong. Yet he discusses how there are times when we must lie to protect people from harm and sometimes just to be polite. Coady also bemoans how "an alarming aspect of so much democratic politics is ... justifying a distressing degree of lying and deception" (2008, 118).

In *Ethics in Light of Childhood* (2010), John Wall bypasses much of the messiness of ethics by viewing problems through the eyes and abilities of children. Luckily, most children are not as torn down by everyday tensions as adults. Our responsibility to the young is to nurture creativity, to encourage expansion of their narratives, and to ask them to respond to otherness. "To be moral, in light of childhood, is to construct and reconstruct social meaning over time and in response to one another" (Wall 2010, 179). "The difference between children and adults is ... a matter of degree rather than kind" (Wall 2010, 176).

The truth is, everyone lies. It is practical to choose to lie rarely and thoughtfully. We tell this to children. When the bad guy asks which way the good guy ran, you lie. Where to begin? By telling our stories and then expanding them so that they become more responsive to others—including creative views of our needs and wants.

Rights and Responsibilities

As we become adolescents, our rights and responsibilities are entwined. Ethical behavior is dependent on responsible actions. What hopefully develops in the interaction is a personal history of agency—growing out of behaviors that demonstrate desired accomplishments. The feeling of personal power derived from actions is likely to lead to success. Accompanying this feeling is a sense of agency that can spread to other areas of endeavor. There is cause to believe that defending one's rights makes sense from the view of the mind and heart. A nuanced practice of ethics aims at maintaining everyone's integrity. Winning and losing are not the only criteria of success. A preponderance of success is most helpful.

As guides for these young people, we must set up situations in which small amounts of success can substantially accrue—moving from relatively easy examples to increasingly more challenging problems. We must avoid discussions that do not exemplify authentic agency. It is damaging to lead discussions that use democratic methods in a context represented by a less-than-sufficient balance of power. We must not hold up the possibility of real success when there is little chance of truly satisfying the rights that children claim. Inauthentic work is a breeding ground for young cynicism. Agency brings an increase in trust and hope. Responsiveness to others must grow as children's social worlds expand alternatives for both themselves and others together. The notions of what is right and of rights are also entwined. The voices of the young warrant attentive consideration.

The Rights of War and Peace

The following story (Henderson 2006) is based on one etched in cuneiform on Sumerian clay tablets and summarized here to illustrate the very ancient history of concern for resolving dangerous political dilemmas—incorporating myth and some reality.

The story of Lugalbanda, the oldest story yet recorded in the world, recounts how a conflict between the right of a king to make war and the right of the people of Aratta to have peace is resolved by expanding the narrative into a larger worldview. All this happens to real and not so real people woven into an adventure that has served as a template for countless children's books over the last five thousand years. The main characters are King Enmerkar of Uruk; young Prince Lugalbanda and his seven older brothers; Inana, the goddess of love and war; and Anzu, a magical bird. The story revolves around the courageous young Lugalbanda, who faces great dangers to bring to King Enmerkar, with the help of Anzu and the wisdom of Inana, a message that resolves the conflict. In the end, the king takes home to Uruk all the riches he desires, and the people of Aratta are honored and left in peace.

King Enmerkar is included in a Sumerian king list that has survived on another clay tablet. Lugalbanda becomes the king who succeeds him. Most real about this story is the message. King Enmerkar is instructed to restore to its original beauty the city of Aratta, which has been greatly damaged by a year of war. He then learns from the artisans of Aratta how they make the great treasures he desires so that he can take these skills home to be taught to the artisans of Uruk. The story was retranslated in 2006 CE into a children's book by Kathy Henderson, who "tried to stay true to the spirit" of the original text. Some of the cuneiform symbols were missing on the stone tablets, leaving gaps in the translation she used. She used her intuition and creativity to fill in the blanks.

Text Box 2.4 The First Textbooks

Compare the story of *Lugalbanda* by Kathy Henderson (2006) with the following discussion of *History Begins at Sumer* by Samuel Kramer (1981).

Sam Kramer was an archeology professor who lived during most of the twentieth century. Because of him and many other archeologists who liked to dig up ancient clay tablets from the ruins of modern-day Iraq and learned how to read the ancient wedge-shaped cuneiform symbols, which were not exactly hieroglyphics or letters, the story of Lugalbanda was uncovered and translated. We can think of Sam as the first Indiana Jones.

On other clay tablets, Kramer found evidence of the first moral ideals: "The Sumerians, according to their own records, cherished goodness and truth, law and order, justice and freedom, righteousness and straightforwardness, mercy and compassion" (1981, 101); "Kings and rulers constantly boasted of the fact that they had ... wiped out evil and violence" (1981, 102).

Kramer also found artifacts that gave us a picture of the first schools, including textbooks and compositions written by students. One student wrote that "he had to take canings, from various members of the school staff for such indiscretions as talking, standing up, and walking out of the gate" (Kramer 1981, 11). The student was particularly upset when a scribe caned him because his etching (handwriting) was unsatisfactory.

What sense do you make of the conflict embedded in these two reports of life in these ancient times? How do they apply to your life today?

CHAPTER 3

CONVERSATION

We have already established that lecturing and preaching are not enough to assure that students will both learn about and practice ethics. For this to fully take place, there have to be thought-provoking and sufficiently stimulating conversations to aid the development of a common vocabulary. Teachers and students working together can make this happen.

Out of this work, commitment to the values of community can grow. Discussing the elements of ethics and how dilemmas can be resolved builds a stronger understanding and becomes the foundation. As it becomes more and more substantial, the process recreates for students their social world while slowly affecting their connections with the larger world in which they live. Conversation as a concept needs to be an essential partner in the practical framework that supports teaching and learning ethics. It is a process that leads to honoring commitments.

With willingness among teachers and students to participate in the dialogue with open minds, with students hopefully rising up to assert leadership at times and all contributing to an expansion of the narrative, the intellectual and emotional ground will be fertile for all involved. The narrative is a positive influence on the ethical community that is developing—in class, at home, and in the surrounding world.

Discussion, Not Preaching

While Jerry and Frank Griswold, a retired Episcopal bishop, were discussing this chapter over lunch, Frank added (preached?) a few words (a sermonette?) of his own:

> The words "conversation" and "conversion" come from the same Latin root—meaning, "to turn." Conversation can therefore expand our perceptions, alter our points of view, and oblige us to turn our minds and hearts in a new direction. Conversation, if entered into with openness and receptivity, can be costly because it involves risk. It is the risk of being changed by the encounter with another.

"I could go on," he said, but he didn't—not wanting to be pedantic and repetitive. Both men are good talkers and good listeners, and Jerry reported how much they enjoyed their lunch together.

Overall, the study of ethics requires conversation that includes thinking, talking, listening, and, most importantly, hearing with an openness to change. Ethical knowledge is more than a set of rules. Developing an understanding of ethics and learning to behave ethically are communal efforts.

Opportunities to articulate our own thinking and discover that what we say is understood bring ethics to life (Dewey 1909; Simon 2001). The goal is to grow with others in ways that reflect change in each and every one who is participating. Learning by oneself has its rewards, but they are not sufficient. Good conversation demands relationship with others and mutual understandings. More than the words we read and think about alone, words spoken with others have a manifold increase in impact. There can be great joy and substance in building knowledge together.

Our experience leads us to believe that all ethical considerations can benefit from discussion and that learning in community is more likely to lead to fruitful actions. The goal is to expand understanding in ways that allow divergent points of view to coexist within a common narrative—to achieve mutual understanding that comes closer to a meeting of minds (Kidder 1995, 2005). The study of ethics and the practice of ethics are much the same thing. Ethics is an interaction of the many aspects of our lives (Dewey 1909; Horton and Freire 1990).

Many remember Myles Horton and Paulo Freire, authors of *We Make the Road by Walking* (1990) and two great educators of the twentieth century, for their moral courage. Freire, a Brazilian, was acclaimed for his teachings that helped to liberate the oppressed in his country. Though less in the limelight than his students, Horton was director of the Highlander Folk School in Tennessee for training in the arts of resistance. Martin Luther King Jr. and Rosa Parks (before her refusal to go to the back of the bus) were his students, among many others.

In *We Make the Road by Walking,* these two great men talk at length with each other—sharing and comparing their lives' work. Myles tells a scary story about when one member of a group of strikers ironically threatened to shoot him if he did not tell them how to plan a forceful nonviolent action.

The obvious question is, What would you do in Horton's place? But more relevant to a young person, in our view, is the story of Mia's bravery at the end of chapter 1 in this volume, when she confronts her whole class with, "Guys, we have to admit ..."

Spontaneous Conversation

It was the spring of 1965. We were living in Oxford, Ohio, home of Miami University, where Jerry was teaching. Northern civil rights workers, in response to a call from Dr. Martin Luther King Jr. and others, were stopping on their way to Selma for a march to Montgomery, the capital of Alabama. A local committee of concerned citizens in Oxford had offered to provide for the marchers coming through. They would need food and lodging for the night.

Donna called Mrs. Johnson to set a time for a committee meeting. Knowing that she had two small children, as did Donna, she suggested that they meet in the evening when their husbands could be home or, if necessary, when it was easiest to get a student to babysit. "Oh no," she said, "I have a young teenager too, and it's he I *have* to be home for in the evening."

She explained that coming back from wherever, the little ones would run up and spurt out how they felt and exactly what they had been doing while she was away. With her teenage son, it was important to be around throughout the evening. If he was going to talk, it would be around the time he was getting ready for bed, but only if she had been in the house the whole the time. It didn't happen every night, but with patience, she would be there when he needed her. If something was bothering him or he was curious about other kinds of worries, ideas, or feelings, it was worth the wait. Most evenings, though, nothing was said.

Many children this age are not prone to talk. Mrs. Johnson taught Donna the ethical importance being available for spontaneous conversations.

A Common Vocabulary

Adult leadership is needed to guide and discover what kinds of conversations are fruitful for young people (Goodman and Lesnick 2001; Nucci 2001; Power 2002; Shumaker and Heckel 2007). What we lecture about, what we ask them to read or do, and how we ask them to behave become the content for their discussions with adults and each other. The first task is finding what works to build a common vocabulary for talking about ethics. Many of the key words we have been using in this text are expected to compel children's interest. A word like "messy" is plain and often part of confrontational talk; energy is bound up in the word. The same is true for the concept of children's rights. Other words, like "laws" and "rules," embody familiar concepts. "Compassion," as we have said, is not common, but many other words describe it and easily lead to its active use in a discussion. "Right versus right" is typically a new idea; yet recognition of its plain meaning encounters few obstacles. "Dilemma" is similar.

The possibility of using the vocabulary found in young people's books, where the stories are compelling, is helpful even if the words have to be isolated within a vocabulary lesson. Sometimes learning big words becomes a challenge greeted with enthusiasm. From their readings, ask children to choose words that puzzle them. Before looking them up or giving the answers, ask students to pool their information in small groups. Often, good answers will emerge with special twists. And if not, students' minds will be well prepared to hear what a teacher has to say.

Enthusiasm is central to the work (Allender 2001). This applies to thinking, talking, and listening. Structures at school and at home must provide time for thinking, make room for those who are not comfortable talking in a group, and set limits for those who take up too much space in a conversation. It takes creativity and cleverness to organize productive discussions that welcome everyone involved. Adults have to develop skills in asserting leadership without being overbearing, and it is better yet when we can also bring out leadership skills in children. Our difficult responsibility is to engage children in thinking about ethics within in a structure where the contributions, though not the same, can be balanced. The conversation certainly is not about adults asking questions and young people answering them. Hopefully, conversations will be interactive and serious, while encouraging no small amount of humor. This is hard work. But we are asking for a similar level of effort from the children.

Text Box 3.1 Hard Work for Adults

The following list samples ethics textbooks already published in the twenty-first century. They are not easy to read or necessarily applicable to every parent or teacher. But they broaden our knowledge of what is needed for an ethics curriculum. In some ways, they are too complicated. And yet, there are gems to be gleaned.

Education in the Moral Domain by Larry Nucci (2001): "A climate of mutual respect and warmth, with fair and consistent application of rules, forms the elemental conditions for an educationally moral atmosphere" (167).
The Moral Stake in Education by Joan Goodman and Howard Lesnick (2001): The task "is to cultivate the *foundations* of a moral identity . . . [but] little is gained by a moral education, indeed any education, that shapes actions without shaping the person" (246; emphasis in original).
Kids of Character by David Shumaker and Robert Heckel (2007): "Recent research . . . suggests that young children are much more perceptive and sophisticated than what was previously thought . . . in regard to their ability to both detect and make decisions about moral issues" (8).

Do you have personal evidence that affirms these assertions?
How might you change your expectations in light of this knowledge?

Guided Discussions

Teachers complain about how certain kids are more than willing to talk than others (Schultz 2003). The problem is blurred by the assumption that this is just the way kids are—some are outgoing, whereas others are shy—and it isn't right to embarrass students by forcing them to speak out. And it's true that forcing them is not right. Setting up discussions that protect opportunities for students to speak their minds requires modifying the style of teaching. The trap in a school setting is imagining that the only format for a discussion is a large group in which everyone is given a chance to participate. Even with this approach, it is possible to prepare students for what they would like to contribute. A teacher can ease a student into making his or her comments at a fitting moment. At home, the story about Mrs. Johnson illustrates both how hard and how easy it can be to have one-on-one talks. She understood how her role in creating a hospitable environment made a significant difference.

Whatever the situation, we have to come to grips with many regular obstacles to conversation (Spooner and Woodcock 2010). One-on-one talks are a good beginning in any situation. They usually work well when a child is asked to talk with another child. Smaller groups in general lower the discomfort of sharing thoughts publicly and increase the likelihood of openness and honesty. This is true particularly when adults are present but not participating directly in the discussions. Small can mean groups of two, four, or eight, depending on circumstances. Once, toward the ending of the Cold War, we led a meeting of Soviet and North American educators in Moscow in 1986. Meeting in an amphitheater with nearly three hundred people, we asked the participants to turn in threes to people either above or below them to form small groups of six. The goal was to find common educational concerns, and the exercise succeeded far beyond our expectations.

Listening

What conversation can accomplish depends on the quality of listening. What children have to say is an important factor, but when their statements go essentially unheard or are not heard well, the value of what was said is lost. When carefully heard, meaning may even

---

Text Box 3.2 Listening

Listening by Katherine Schultz (2003)
Teaching Children to Listen by Liz Spooner and Jacqui Woodcock (2010)

We need to pay attention to Schultz and to Spooner and Woodcock. The former presents a critical framework for teaching across cultural differences. The latter, on the basis of experience, offer a detailed practical approach to developing children's listening skills. Both books address the meaning of silence. When, we ask, does staying quiet turn into being silenced? When does it not?

The Talking Stick

Gather some friends to talk about listening. Use the Native American tradition of forming a circle and speaking only when holding a stick. Any object will do, but a carved wooden cane evokes an ancient tradition and heightens the meaningfulness of the conversation. Everyone in the circle has an opportunity to speak as the talking stick is passed around. Another opportunity arises when it is passed around again.

We add listening to the tradition. Before taking a turn to speak, summarize what was just heard. Be patient and understanding.

be enhanced. To encourage exploration, there needs to be a norm whereby each person's ideas are discussed for a while. The current norm, for adults as well, is to add one disparate idea onto another by immediately going on to another person's thoughts. We encourage a search for a satisfying understanding of each speaker's contribution before moving to another new idea.

Taking time for one person to listen to a partner's ideas and then repeat them back to him or her is a good setup for introducing the work in a group of four, repeating the process of making meaning out of another's contribution. Interest stays lively when the tasks are not drawn out and when rough guidelines set the times allotted to the contribution of each person in a group. No less, an adult participating in a one-on-one conversation with a young person has to make sure that both have fair (not necessarily the same) amounts of time to share their thoughts.

Structures are needed to keep conversations on target and to end them in a timely fashion (Allender 2001). What children read, watch on a big or small screen, and play on a computer all can contribute to the structure if instructions are not too complicated. Brief written work assigned in advance can direct the focus so that everyone has something to offer. It creates the opportunity to ask what we have earlier called true questions—where everyone can contribute relatively easily. None of this guarantees successful leadership. The challenge to accomplish our goals means taking risks. Still, we can learn from failure, and in connection with ethics, we have the opportunity, like the young people themselves, to gain a bit of wisdom if we put in the effort.

Inside and outside school, the value of speaking and listening is intertwined with the development of a sense of capability. More is to be gained for youngsters when they experience their words building into a common understanding with others or, better yet, into an agreed-on course of action (Allender and Allender 2008). If only we adults had more of this kind of experience.

An Urge for Absolutes

The value of children's contributions to a discussion is diminished if questioning adult wisdom is out of the question. If questioning constitutes straying from the path, a child has no personal ground to sustain interest in participating. When tenets are posed that have no possibility of being modified to fit better with an individual's worldview, child or adult, promising to follow the rules isn't grounded in a supportive environment. We see this with people of any age who, when asked to change their behavior, regularly make and then break promises. Efforts become a waste of time and possibly a breeding ground for a personal history of hypocrisy (Emde, Johnson, and Easterbrooks 1987).

So much history, on a worldly scale, has contributed to the development of an ethical canon. In no way, though, has it become a universal body of knowledge. What was once personal knowledge over time turns into canons of belief. Yet this canon, developed over the ages, harbors a multitude of contradictions, points of view, beliefs, and starting points. Unique combinations have functioned in many different cultural contexts. In each present context, the application of ethics requires its own special interpretation.

A legacy of millennia has brought with it an urge for absolutes (Mendieta and VanAntwerpen 2011). And all too often, it is accompanied by strong and intractable feelings. What were once a person's ideas turn into beliefs, over time, so strong that they become worth fighting for and against. When the tenets of ethics are taken as absolute, they limit the potential and generativity of discussion and keep people from engaging in conversations that seek growth and inclusiveness. Dysfunctional conversation stems from expressing this urge; it damages the long-range development of young people by inhibiting the belief that commitment to ethical conversation and corresponding action are worthwhile.

There are naturally gaps between people's ideas and their feelings about others' ideas—between kids and adults as well as among kids. Ethical conflicts begin with these gaps and worsen as communities diverge. With openness, more inclusive community thinking can emerge from an active effort to bridge differences (Blum 1987). This begins with lessening our concerns about being right and heightening efforts to find common ground. Conversations that work toward this bridge are the beginning of further-reaching and more successful commitments (Berkowitz 2002; Etzioni 2002).

Developmental Changes

Developmentally, children's abilities multiply as they grow older. There is, though, a tendency to assume that developmental stages are mainly a set of limitations, and these create expectations narrower than they need to be. How children learn at each stage is different, but this does not necessarily affect what they learn. Ethics is a good example. There is nothing foreign to even young children about considering the difference between right and wrong. Furthermore, all children can think creatively. Creativity is a skill available at any age, and encouraging it reveals infinite possibilities (Wall 2010). Without fixed assumptions, a wider variety of interests and abilities can be expressed. With this more open view of possibilities, there is a chance of finding common ground where children and adults can engage shared interests and concerns together.

Holding young people to high standards is important, but we must recognize that we are contending with different mental organizational structures (Blum 1987; Kegan 1994). At the least, what we want and what we care about are often not the same. Still, we have to stay aware of the fact that becoming an adult entails entry into a world that makes space for hypocrisy and other unethical behaviors. Likewise, young people have conflicting pressures that stimulate tensions between personal needs and social requirements. Young people feel the pressure of peers to stay out later than their curfew while at the same time wanting to obey their parents. Problematic is the fact that adults often imagine that an unforgiving environment will teach children to behave more perfectly than the adults around them have managed. "Do as I say, not as I do" isn't cool in any world.

Between their worldview and ours, complicated by stubbornness all around, we open the relationship to countless failures. Our own honesty and respect make more room for a reciprocal response. For moments, there can be a level playing field—as long as we do not lose sight of our proper authority and responsibility to guide and teach the younger generation. At best, we stand to learn from each other.

Expanding the Narrative

Telling our stories is the heart of ethics. When we asked our friend Jack Whitehead, an educational philosophy professor, about teaching ethics for children becoming adolescents, he said, "I believe that each individual could make a contribution ... by sharing their accounts of how they are working to live ethical principles as fully as possible" (2010). We add, this can be realized by working together. The teaching

---

Text Box 3.3 Social Absolutes

Moral Principles in Education by John Dewey (1909)

"The Science of Character Education" by Marvin Berkowitz (2002)

"In so far as the curriculum is so selected and organized as to provide the material for affording the child a consciousness of the world in which he has to play a part, and the demands he has to meet ... the school is organized on an ethical basis" (Dewey 1909, 44).

Berkowitz reports, "The degree to which children perceive their schools as caring communities is directly related to the effectiveness of those schools in promoting student character development" (2002, 57).

Anyone can declare an absolute—personal, philosophical, psychological, empirical, and even wishful. Some are limiting; others are expanding. Some will exclude and even oppress those who are excluded. Some make room for creative expression. Some make room for greater inclusion. For starters, we like the "right to have rights."

Together or alone, make a list of absolutes in your life. Do any new ones come to mind? Compare them. How do they affect the meaning(s) of ethical behavior?

How do they affect democratic decision making?

How do they encourage the development of moral reasoning?

How do they support caring?

---

of ethics needs to be framed in terms of togetherness. We will actually use different words in what we each say to young people, but the sentiment has to be expressed. What makes the work meaningful is a string of small, reasonable tasks that are likely to meet with success. Out of these tasks arises the self-confidence that supports the efforts involved (see Whitehead 1993).

Adults and children must learn as well to imagine that what others believe and argue is plausible. This attitude makes for talking and listening that express a commitment to thinking and acting ethically. Peter Elbow (1986) proposed, more than twenty-five years ago, "a methodology of belief" for both scientific research and scholarly inquiry in the humanities and social studies. In contrast to the commonly used methodology of doubt, which is a fundamental tenet of Western thought, he invented activities for expanding our narratives by drawing upon opposites. With strong leadership, people are able to fully understand divergent points of view. This requires going beyond superficial agreement and reaching toward authentic common goals. Conversations structured in this manner aim to make communities more inclusive.

Text Box 3.4 Methods of Expanding

Ethics in Light of Childhood by John Wall (2010)
The Growth of Educational Knowledge by Jack Whitehead (1993)
Embracing Contraries by Peter Elbow (1986)

For Wall, children from birth naturally develop by expanding. From birth, children are creative and responsive to others in the service of new possibilities, and so their narratives enlarge. Development is a model for ethical behavior. Whitehead moves the focus to "living theories" and particularly "living contradictions." They reveal how practice is always in flux and therefore an essential opportunity for broadening lives as parents and children, teachers and students, older and younger friends.

Years before, Elbow understood this thinking and how it is possible to use it to teach inclusiveness. We see how youngsters on the cusp of becoming adults might not have to lose this developmental advantage—one that Wall sees as "humanity's ethical purpose ... the expansion rather than the contraction of its own humanity" (2010, 180).

The Believing Game

Arguing a contentious view, introduce a discussion group to three of Elbow's questions as a way of expanding inclusiveness (1986, 275):

- What's interesting or helpful about the view? What are some intriguing features that others might not have noticed?
- What would you notice if you believed this view? If it were true?
- In what senses or under what conditions might this idea be true?

Our experience teaching ethics to junior high students suggests that they are capable of expanding their narratives often more easily than some adults. They rarely have a similar intractability that drives the urge for absolutes. Even youngsters who border on delinquency or worse still have young flexibility that remains in their hearts and minds. Their stories may not justify their behavior, but they can readily explain a worldview that makes sense for them. The expansion of narratives, by these difficult children and other youngsters who are more socially attuned, to include each other is the goal (Blum 1987; Wall 2010).

When describing their experiences, young people should be encouraged to begin, "This is what I believe happened." When they talk about what makes sense to them, they need to be believed. From these starting points, narratives can be expanded to include more responsiveness to others. In common with others, including the older people in their lives, youngsters want to be heard, respected, cared about, valued, and believed. We all want to be recognized as human beings who deserve respect, no matter how different we are. We must encourage wondering about how we can see each other in a good light—if not in many ways, at least in some. This is how ethics becomes a meaningful shared activity in and between communities. Even the people we wish to exclude or lock up should be included in the conversation.

It is valuable for young people to honor and share with each other their disparate points of view. With leadership, help them develop an understanding of how this disparity may have occurred. Also, there is value in noticing what elements of their narratives mesh and how. Most educative might be imagining a grander narrative that includes the disparities—possibly building on the elements that already mesh. We do need our differences, and we need to live in a community that does not trample on each other's liveliness.

SECTION TWO

Practical Applications

INTRODUCTION TO SECTION TWO

The curriculum moves forward with exploration and practice. There is teaching to do—about confronting bullies, building an ethical classroom community, demonstrating a personal work ethic, and finding ways to participate in addressing more global concerns. Each presents unique questions about ethical behavior. Some will become obvious with discussion; others will emerge from creative thinking. The teacher's job is to tap the intrinsic energy of students with experiential activities that challenge them, connect with their excitement, and promise to be doable by the students in a short enough time. A track record of small successes that build confidence for the teacher and the students is needed. It is no small matter for both to take on such an awesome task as expecting children becoming adolescents to tackle a course in ethics.

We began with bullying because it was from this that there emerged a need and indeed a demand for the course. In our minds, it wasn't enough just to quell the bullying. This had to happen first, but, overall, we believed that students needed to understand the larger context. We connected our work with tensions that had touched all of them in some way—as perpetrators, victims, or those too frightened to act. B. Coloroso (2008) argues that "the bully, the bullied, and the bystander" are each playing roles. She adds that the roles are not immutable so that finding ways to change are not necessarily impossible and herein lies the challenge. Understanding what underlies the roles can lead to an increase in agency for at least getting help. With know-how and luck, students can even become a part of making the peace.

The second topic focused on community building. Education from our point of view is most effective in a well-functioning community (Allender and Allender 2008). It seems obvious to say so, but we must understand that everyday reality makes the goal hard work and sometimes complex. This was certainly the case when we announced that the regular curriculum would immediately be modified to confront the breakdown of a connected social environment.

On our side we had a history of classroom work that involved children in meaningful projects accomplished as a group. In other semesters, there had been great success putting on plays, producing a student-written school newspaper, working toward class trips, linking ecology with art, and completing other projects linking academic work with artistic expression. Though growing out of stressful diversity, we were able to work together with positive, intriguing goals ahead. We were actually not surprised to find that children prefer a productive learning environment that is not stressful. Studying ethics, like all others, wove together reading, writing, and discussion with experiential activities on a daily basis. We built community by working together to achieve common goals.

The third topic focused on the improvement of classwork and homework. We were not satisfied with the quality of the children's writing and turned our dissatisfaction into educating them in a work ethic. It is not a kind of ethic that one can expect to find in a text about children's moral or character development, but it is a topic of academic concern, as evidenced by a nearly century-old discussion initiated in *The Protestant Ethic and the Spirit of Capitalism* by Max Weber (1930). Weber's focus had much to do with economics and sociology, but his writing also provides an understanding of the expectations set for students in Western culture.

Our expectations are clearly related to a humanistic educational subculture, but no less, we expect accomplishments that stand up to public adult judgment. This expectation was realized when the final expression of the students' work became an ethics exhibit displayed in two local coffeehouses. In a small but significant way, their work was acclaimed by the school's teachers, the children's parents, regulars in the coffee shops, and children from their school and other schools. This is no small accomplishment.

Finally, we broadened our horizon to encompass global concerns. Local ones were included, but there were no geographical limits on where else in the world to choose to pay attention. Having a copy of *The Teen Guide to Global Action: How to Connect with Others (Near and Far) to Create Social Change* (Lewis 2008) was immeasurably helpful. The guide was thought provoking, filled with examples, and supportive of engaging active learning and practical challenges. Again, school history was helpful. The ethical value of participating in community work was already clear to the students. This kind of work was a regular part of their curriculum. Knowing the importance of ethical behavior in this sphere didn't preclude bullying in the daily school environment, but once confronted and engaged in the study of ethics, they could see how the two relate to each other—or, one might say, do not relate to each other.

Curriculum Outline

The four topics outlined were not always taught in a linear fashion. They were interwoven with the theoretical discussions as they promised to fit together. The reality of everyday teaching always entails following a plan while contending with a host of interruptions. Some are annoying; others are chosen because a direction too good to miss presents itself. The curriculum is important, but more valuable is how well ethics is understood and practiced at the end of the day.

Chapter 4: Fear is the first order of business. Bullies work at making others afraid of them. The discussion then turns to the leadership required to undo this fear. This includes a set of techniques that can be practiced, like role-playing, in the classroom. We also address the question, What can parents (and grandparents) do?

Wonder by R. J. Palacio (2012) is first on our list for truly understanding bullying. We didn't have a chance to use it in class because it was yet to be published. Painful to read, though funny at times, it came to our attention in a *New York Times* book review and again from a prepublication copy lent by our friend, Alyson Silverman, a children's librarian who was on the lookout for us for books that confronted ethical problems. She somehow knew how important *Wonder* was. We include a mini review. That it will be assigned in the future is a given.

Chapter 5: The key text is *Aikido in Action* by Terry Dobson (1983). A powerful story, it leads to a discussion of building community with the major example of the students' own classroom, the role of families and their values, community projects, and an analysis of "ethics in the light of a junior high community."

Chapter 6: We found no good book focusing primarily on work ethic in children. But *E Is for Ethics* by Ian Corlett (2009) suffices. Better as a text that covers a wide scope of ethical concerns, it includes a few stories that relate to the development of the application of intrinsic effort and commitment. This discussion is related to the potential of small groups in elementary school and projects that bring out enthusiasm.

Chapter 7: *The Teen Guide to Global Action* (Lewis 2008) serves to connect the discussion about a widespread concern for global action with engaging the participation of students in doing something about global concerns. We present activities that can be done in- or outside class on a larger scale.

CHAPTER 4

THE MANY FACES
OF BULLYING

When bullying becomes news, we already know two things: (1) there has been an unattended history of bullying, and (2) inadequate attention has been paid to the context in which the bullying is occurring. When there was an outbreak of bullying in the junior high at the Project Learn School, we immediately knew that multiple social dynamics required examination, beginning with the roles that both children and adults play. Everyone involved, including bystanders—the community as a whole—needed to be held accountable.

But first, caveat emptor. Much of what has been written about bullying conveys something akin to a misplaced fascination with bullies and their victims. This is why it is news. However, we must not shy away from placing blame if it is clear where it belongs. It is essential to pinpoint responsibility—or, more accurately, irresponsibility. And it is essential to redress wrongs done to victims.

Bullying entails more than one big child threatening or acting violently with one or more smaller children. Someone who is blustering, quarrelsome, and overbearing and who badgers and intimidates weaker people is without doubt a bully. But intimidation has many forms: teasing, taunting, slandering, exclusion from a rightful place in the community, othering with racial and sexual slurs, and threats of all kinds are part of the problem. Anything meant to hurt or intimidate another, done by one person or many, counts. Sometimes this is true even when intent is missing. And most often, what looks simply like bullying is more complex than it appears (Allender and Allender 2001; Coloroso 2008; Rigby 2008; Sullivan 2000).

There are many ways to hurt others, but the predominant tactic of the bully is to instill fear. There are other ways to infringe on the rights of others, but fear puts young people on a worse footing for learning how to get along. Clear leadership is necessary to alleviate the fear and to guide the victim and the bully to an equitable reconciliation. This chapter aims to provide teachers with sufficient information to create a curriculum that ameliorates and helps prevent bullying.

An Outbreak of Bullying

At dinner one evening, early in the school year, Donna talked about an outbreak of bullying in the junior high at the Project Learn School. This was shocking. We appreciated that there was no physical violence involved. But this small school, with fewer than one hundred students in any given year, is known in Philadelphia, around the country, and in other places in the world for a humanistic philosophy that captures the hearts of the parents who run the school, the teachers who are delighted for the opportunity to teach there, and the children who love

---

Text Box 4.1 I Was a Bully

"Gestalt Theory for Teachers" by Jerome S. Allender and Donna Sclarow Allender (2001)

Soon after we were married (in 1958), Jerry told me one night at dinner about how his teaching had gone that day. Two junior high students had been so incorrigible, he had pressed one against the blackboard with his knee and squeezed the other in a tight grip. I imagine he glared at them. For him, there was a truce. But not for me. Out of my depths came, "Don't you ever do that again." Sometimes a strong authoritative voice makes a difference. Leadership comes in many forms. "OK," Jerry said, and then we talked.

We learned a lot that evening. A fine theoretician and a good enough teacher, Jerry had a lot to discover about practice. His anger came from his own fear that he was unable to control these boys. Forty years later, we had more confidence and a better understanding: "An awareness of fears makes them less figural, gives teachers more creative self-control, and supports an openness for contact" (Allender and Allender 2001, 135). Contact means a connection with another individual that engenders change in both people.

Were you ever a bully?

Were you ever bullied?

Maybe not. Find someone who was—it's not hard.

Deep knowledge of bullying begins with these experiences.

coming to school every morning. Though problems found in schools everywhere arise there, an "outbreak of bullying" was unusual and disturbing.

Project Learn is a community where members of all ages are expected to work together cooperatively. The breakdown of respect is everyone's business. No one is excused—including the two of us. Among the founders of Project Learn forty years ago, Donna, along with Fran Fox and Nancy Bailey, were teacher-parents who led this parent-cooperative K–8 school. Our children graduated, and then came the grandchildren. Donna retired in the early 1990s to become a psychotherapist, but in recent years, with our own grandson enrolled, she began helping out as an assistant teacher and serving on the administrative committee. Jerry did staff development and worked as an assistant teacher.

We witnessed none of the instances. We were bystanders with a history of active involvement. Teachers talked of slurs about homosexuality, text messages with inappropriate sexual content ostensibly sent by a child who didn't send them, and an assigned Halloween paper for English that detailed how each teacher in the school would die. This all began with a misguided democratic process for choosing who would stay in which bunk during an overnight end-of-school camping trip, one that would have left one child to sleep in a cabin alone. It was nice to know that a classmate stepped up and changed his choice. Both were ostracized and pelted with homophobic slurs by the biggest bully.

For some time before the bullying incident, we had been witnessing ruder behavior between children and adults than we had seen before. We worried about a lack of the structure that young people should be expected to live and learn within. There needs to be leeway, but not so loose that critical behaviors are excused. We talked. Donna met with the junior high teachers, Jerry met with one of the teachers who despaired most, and out of these talks we planned an ethics course for the two junior high classes.

Taking Charge

Jerry met with the junior high students to introduce the course. They didn't object to the plan, except for the fact that the ethics class would meet during the special times during the week reserved for a promised course based on their own interests. It was to be a special kind of "elective." They complained bitterly about this. "Why couldn't one of our regular courses be canceled to make time?" Jerry calmly and firmly told them that they were not required to like it, just to participate and do the work. The students challenged his ethics, because the course had arbitrarily been imposed in a school where the child's needs are professed to come first. "You temporarily lost your right to choose."

They are good kids. They saw that there was a job to be done—to learn more about ethics and to put into practice a more complete understanding. They recognized that this was not punishment and that these were reasonable consequences. We recognize the gift of such a beginning. Most kids are not bad. A lot has to do with their sense of safety and their needs being met sufficiently. There has to be a level of respect for each individual; no one expects to get everything he or she wants. We are thankful that daily classroom behavior at Project Learn has never come close to the terrors we know others experience. We don't know exactly what we would do in extreme circumstances. But what happened at the school is how most kinds of bullying begin. We must not wait until it gets worse. This is more than bad enough.

Ken Rigby, in his book *Children and Bullying* (2008), distinguishes between nonmalign and malign bullying. Sometimes kids horse around. Sometimes there can be a middle ground. And then there is outright bullying. He lists what we have to watch out for: the use of greater, aggressive power; when kids want to hurt someone or do; when threats are made; when actions taken are not provoked in any way; and when there are feelings of oppression or perpetrators announce how they enjoy domination. Gestures, words, and physical force all count. It is a good list—not perfect, but helpful.

At Project Learn, the teachers differed in their perceptions of the severity of the problem of the bullying. Ironically, the children agreed on the value of an ethics course, if not with what it would replace in the weekly schedule. Our call was based on what had transpired over several months—coupled with incidences of overt malign bullying.

The two of us asked a single question: Were teachers and students primarily working together or against each other? Against, we agreed, and decided that a community intervention was needed. No one was entirely happy with our offer to teach an ethics course, but on different levels, all agreed to cooperate. Good enough.

Leadership

The story must include the actions of someone in charge (Shulman 2004). A response must not be hindered by waiting for full exploration of the circumstances. The story must immediately be interrupted and changed. Guided by intuitive knowledge, someone has to respond in a way that demonstrates firm and responsive leadership. It would be great if a child were to do this. But there has to be a public display of concern, clarity, and belief that consequences will follow.

The tension between reflection and action is not resolvable. This tension underlies the meaning of leadership. An environment that implicitly condones bullying, or even the appearance of bullying that turns out to be benign, is lined with potholes at best; it is a minefield at worst. It is not as if adults have all the answers. At stake is the ability to cope with ambiguity and the competence to model for young people what they need to learn. A story of bullying can look less like bad behavior, with successful leadership, and more like an opportunity. Bullying can be turned around in the process of the confrontation. What looks like bullying doesn't have to harden into a sensational event that becomes an item of bad news for a newspaper.

There are the elements of successful confrontation: employing the power of authority, speaking out strongly, using techniques of mediation, and transforming injustices into a community problem (Swearer, Espelage, and Napolitano 2009). Sometimes it is most useful for adults to work individually with bullies with the aim of substantially changing their behavior. A bully might be capable of and ready for this transformation. With sensitivity, victims can become smarter and more confident in handling difficulties that confront them. There are possibilities for helping a victim and a bully to resolve injustice on their own. There is always more to learn that can broaden our understanding of what has happened and what might be done to address and redress the situation. Importantly, a community that learns to resolve problems on its own, not necessarily with adult involvement, can best bring all of this together. In the process, everyone has something at stake and something to learn.

A sense of the larger context must take into account that adult life is rife with unethical behavior (Lichtenberg 1990; Lichtenberg, van Beusekom, and Gibbons 1997). This is a significant component of the model the adult world sets for children. Only blinders could possibly let us forget that a large part of life includes cruelty. Every child on earth inherits this legacy. From time immemorial, humans, more than any other species, have treated each other in cruel ways. Nothing we do can hide this from young people. Every day, much of what we speak about, publish in the newspaper, show on television, and post online teaches the young that expectations of them differ from what they read, hear, and see. Demanding that children be holier than we are—less tolerant of their mistakes than our own—will likely exacerbate problems and diminish the desire to demonstrate cooperative social behavior. We have to be humbled by the big picture and not expect more of children than we can model in our own lives.

The smart strategy for adults, teachers, parents, and anyone else is to interweave kindness with the firm requirement for acceptable behavior. The details of this smaller local context can become a story of change that leads to an improved life for the community. As problems get more complex, the goal is to simplify them and get on with the productive and fun part of being a community. We paint this kind of rosy picture because it represents the best of our experience and the hope we maintain for the lives of children growing up. Contrary to imagining that zero tolerance and holding to hard lines are the best ways to teach children ethics, we see the real world as more nuanced for people of all ages. There even exist national and international rights for children that support the opportunity to learn how to live ethically (Wall 2010). In the long run, an open attitude is in their interest and ours. Standards of cooperative social behavior can be maintained, along with a mutual awareness of room for negotiating differences of opinion.

The Anti-bullying Handbook by Keith Sullivan argues how often studies "tend to generalize about the components of the bullying dynamic, to make judgments about the individuals involved, and to deal more with the components [roles] than the whole system" (2000, 4). In contrast, his "perspective recognizes that bullying is a serious problem, and it aims to work hard to find solutions that improve everyone's chances, both the bully and the bullied" (Sullivan 2000, 4). In her book *The Bully, the Bullied, and the Bystander* (2008), Barbara Coloroso uses the roles of the bully, the bullied, and the bystander "to identify only a role that a child is performing at that moment, in that one scene of one act in a longer play. It is not intended to define or permanently label a child. The goal is to gain a clearer understanding of these roles and how the interactions involved in such role playing . . . are not healthy, not normal, and certainly not necessary and in fact can be devastating to children playing any of the three characters" (4–5).

We found children and adults who remembered both bullying and being bullied, as well as bystanders who today carry regrets for not having acted to protect a friend. There are children who have acted and succeeded in helping. There are also those who feel otherwise about what happened. A sense of agency can change and turn around the meaning of a bad event, because it is within the power of the players to complain, to change, and to learn how to get along better.

However much we discuss the big picture and its nuances, however much we need to develop methods for coping with bullying and the introduction of antibullying programs, something must be done first to immediately stop the behavior. This is the zero tolerance. Acts of bullying must stop now! Then the consequences for the bully or the bullies are subject to discussion, and these discussions must eschew zero tolerance so that workable solutions can be found. The bully must suffer consequences, if possible without exclusion from the community.

Discussions about preventing bullying, problem solving, and exploring and demanding responsibility must take place in an emotional and intellectual climate where the bullying has first been stopped. This is where adults have to take charge or find someone with the social or physical power to halt the hurtful actions. The most powerful response in the long run is found in the use of words that command. Earning this power is what becoming a responsible adult is about in an important way. This is how we model thinking about and practicing ethics.

Bullying 101

As teachers, we have to help our children figure out strategies for responding creatively (Ludwig 2010; Palacio 2012). Are there ways to undermine bullying before it escalates dangerously? What might be options for confronting a bully? What can one do as an observer of bullying? How might a bully learn to have and apply some self-awareness?

The introduction to the unit on bullying was a lecture based on a shortened version of this discussion so far. Students were invited to share their thoughts, reactions, and creative possibilities. As a counterpoint, Susan Deutsch, a parent at Project Learn and a movement educator, was asked to introduce a bullying exercise where talking was ruled out. During this exercise, no conversation and no touching were allowed.

The activity began with students in pairs seated face to face, not talking, not touching, with their feet on the floor. With only the upper part of the body, they were to move their hands, arms, torso, and heads—using body language to communicate—with a special emphasis on using bold and creative facial expressions as much as possible. They were even allowed to threaten physical violence. The task was to create a problem between the two of them and resolve it in the space of five minutes. Students were drawn in by the craziness of the task and its obvious poignancy. It was funny and instructive. The students' experiences demonstrated how creative behaviors could possibly de-escalate tensions. We all knew they were not sure bets, but our minds were opened to searching for such moves.

A high-spirited and insightful discussion followed the experience. The students understood that this was not what would happen in real life, but the activity elevated the talk to a thoughtful ethical conversation about possibilities that they hadn't thought of before this class. They realized the difference between actions that created (or expressed) fear and those that created contact. These possibilities were within their grasp.

Text Box 4.2 How Little We Know

Bullying Prevention and Intervention by Susan Swearer, Dorothy Espelage, and Scott Napolitano (2009)

Swearer, Espelage, and Napolitano ask, "Is there a need for another book about bullying?" They answer that despite a huge increase in writing and research about bullying over the last thirty years, "we still don't have very good solutions about what to do about bullying, how to stop bullying, or more realistically, how to reduce bullying behavior among school-age children" (ix).

In response to their worries, they have written a thorough report that can serve as a starting point in a wide range of contexts. They cover children of all ages and pay attention to the individual, peer group, school, family, and community. The report heightens awareness of social conditions that aggravate day-to-day relationships and includes a variety of case studies, strategies for developing policy, attention to legal issues, and realistic plans to reduce bullying. It also considers the impact of technology on bullying and ways to think about evaluation. The report is an excellent resource that itself points to many other resources.

Swearer, Espelage, and Napolitano clarify that for all they have learned, each unique sphere within which bullying appears requires careful attention. With their knowledge and so many other resources that have served us in our work, we have created, and continue to create, ever-new possibilities for guiding the children, teachers, and parents we encounter.

Role-Playing

Role-playing also has the potential for shifting children's minds (Allender 2001). There are various ways to set it up. Situations can be based on personal experience, where students have the opportunity to replay what didn't work—to say what they wish they had said. They can be based on stories that children have heard or on readings that stimulate experimental possibilities. And they can be creative adventures into behaviors that at first seem outside their repertoire. Children can experiment with expressing anger in a controlled way, or they might not use words at all and instead stare into the aggressor's eyes, reflecting a hidden power. This creativity brings a larger range of behaviors into view.

Asking children to act out different ways of reacting in a situation with a bully evokes a variety of feelings. These can be queried and coached. Playing the victim, a student is instructed to acquiesce to the bully who says, "Give me your lunch money." How does that feel? In a replay, students might engage the bully in talk. "What's up? Are you hungry?" "No money for lunch?" What is that like? Again, students can imagine deceiving a bully. "I've got money in my locker." The intention is to move the bully to a place where the victim can get help. Another is to resist. "I am going to tell my parents or my teacher if I give you money. Even if you threaten me or hurt me, someone still is going to know." We believe this will give students a sense of strength.

Another set of alternatives for role-playing can respond to the more typical ways in which girls bully. One can search for a variety of responses to statements intended to humiliate, such as, "Your skirt is really ugly." Without the context in which behaviors like these actually unfold, responses in the role-playing can border on or become a farce. Yet all of this play, as it can be called, does loosen up potentially useful responses in the event of a real confrontation. Subtleties abound. Maybe the confrontation is nothing more than "That skirt's out of style," and yet the comment hurts. Certainly, all the little plays are grist for serious conversation.

Bottom line, protecting oneself from violence is key. It's a good thing to measure the risk involved. Children who are studying karate have a better shot. It is helpful that their discipline comes with a strong emphasis on avoiding violence. It gets toughest when a bully is only out to hurt someone. Truth be told, there might not be a role-playing situation to anticipate the worst; there might be opportunities for learning, though, in replaying a bad experience with both a hardened bully and a badly hurt victim. Sometimes the scenario is too hard to imagine, and role-playing is not the answer.

Art

A mix of writing and drawing opens another world to the deepening of understanding; this mode of expression can teach us how to communicate peacefully and powerfully. However much one might mistakenly disregard art as less than central to children's learning, it has been poignantly significant in our teaching. One activity began with the question, What is a bully? We used the answers to construct a web of words on a four-by-eight-foot poster. The web is a kind of picture that represents a thorough definition, even if not derived from academic considerations, of a bully. Then, each student illustrated his or her contribution to the web on a smaller poster.

Shayma offered, "Closed in." She drew, with a set of marking pens, a colorful young man with outrageous hair, not quite realistic but in your face. His chest exposed his heart in bright red—trapped behind a black iron grate that one might find on the window of a prison cell. Though Shayma recognized that the drawing accurately conveyed what she knew and felt, the primitive artwork embarrassed her. It was not up to the standards she had developed with her art teacher. A discussion of the valued role of primitive artists in the art world convinced her to allow us to show it here.

What Can Parents Do?

When trouble surfaces and a child says something to an adult outside school, and the school is not doing enough, what options empower us as adults and empower children? Make time and think creatively. Begin by listening empathetically, not only to a victim or a bystander but even to a culprit.

Photo 4.1 Draw a Bully

Hear the story, enter into it, and become a character who changes its course. Optimally, confronting bullying will turn into a conversation that responds to the needs and wants of everyone involved—in the classroom, in the home, or in the street. The reality is often hard and painful (Coloroso 2008; Rigby 2008; Sullivan 2000).

An effective response has to break a lot of mind-sets. A relevant question is, How do we change negative behaviors into those that nurture positive social behavior? We hope to find allies among other parents, teachers, administrators, and our children's friends. Our friend, Kathe Telingator, did take action as a parent when she discovered that her daughter was the target of cyberbullying. She contacted the parents of the bullies and organized a meeting of all the children and their parents. Together they sorted out what had happened, sincere apologies were made, and the bullying behavior stopped (Telingator 2007).

It doesn't always happen that way. Sometimes potential friends turn out to be enemies. Start by being more connected with your youngsters. Have regular connections with other parents. Be helpful to teachers. Gather allies. Generate conversation. Amass some political power. On a larger scale, it is like making peace instead of war. Work together, and hope for the best.

Activities involving movement exercises, role-playing, and art could take place, with a bit of pushiness and humor, at home. From the example above, we see that it may not be so difficult to bring together children in a setting outside school. This can help level the playing ground and get at problems without the complication of having teachers about. In a bullying incident, remember that it is valuable for all children involved to be gathered together to talk. Assess whether you have the skills to lead such a discussion. Be aware that ineffective leadership can make things worse.

When each child tells her or his take on what happened, it might be possible to establish a sense of responsibility. The adult needs to confront publicly the child who has been bullying for the sake of the bullied child or children. This establishes a path for potentially making amends. Bullying most often happens in secret with threats of revenge for disclosure. The gathering of the children with a responsible adult undermines the secrecy.

The advantage of working with children before they are fully adolescent is that they are likely to be less guarded and less entrenched in new habits that are forming. There may be little spaces where vulnerability makes for more openness. As adults, we need to rise to the personal challenge by matching our own vulnerability with theirs. As always, this in no way means we give up our proper authority as adults. We just don't let our self-importance make us think we are smarter than we really are. It's a matter of modeling openness as a way of connecting. If a problem turns out not to be bullying, likely something else is troublesome. Breakdowns in the social fabric need to be addressed. Social environments of every kind are like mobiles with their rods, wires, and artistic objects; when one part moves, everything else in the system moves.

The Karate Kid

Sometimes children younger than junior high age have thoughtful answers to questions too. Donna asked Dylan, our grandson, then nine, "What makes someone a bully?" He answered, "They have mean parents." This is not the only answer, but it strikes at the heart.

Text Box 4.3 Two Stories

Confessions of a Former Bully by Trudy Ludwig (2010)
Wonder by R. J. Palacio (2012)

In *Confessions*, Katie the bully narrates. In *Wonder*, August is bullied, and often he is the narrator. Sometimes it is Jack, his best friend, who betrays him, or Summer, a steadfast, trusted friend, or Olivia, or Justin.

Katie tells her story like a curriculum. Roles are clarified: there are the bully, teachers, parents, bystanders, and a counselor. Katie changes. Big values are emphasized: caring, friendship, listening, and practical advice.

Wonder is dramatic. At one point, August says, "Rat boy. Freak. Freddy Krueger. E.T. Gross-out. Lizard face. Mutant. I know the names they call me. I've been in enough playgrounds to know kids can be mean. I know, I know, I know" (Palacio 2012, 79). August's face is badly deformed. Children and adults recoil. Be vulnerable, and the story will touch your heart.

As August and Jack whisper about a mix of slug juice and dog pee to spray at bullies, the teacher reprimands them for disturbing the class. Then Jack whispers, "Are you always going to look this way, August? I mean, can't you get plastic surgery or something?" August smiles and points to his face. "Hello? This is after plastic surgery!" Jack claps his hand over his forehead and starts laughing hysterically. "Dude, you should sue your doctor!" (64).

Older children can teach *Confessions* to younger ones. *Wonder* can connect children with adults. Both books are winners.

Another time, he and I were talking on the way to his karate class. We were comparing the two kinds of sensei portrayed in the movie *The Karate Kid*. It was clear to us that his own sensei was all about "peace and friendship," as they say regularly in each lesson, not winning by cheating.

"What about bullying?" I asked. He was clear: "First, I would try to find an adult. If I didn't, I'd think about my chances, and then I would deck him." I have to admit, I felt proud. As a grandfather, I was clear. As a teacher and once a parent of more than one nine-year-old, I still have some thinking to do. My pride aside, I also know that violence does not resolve violence.

CHAPTER 5

COMMUNITY ETHICS

We begin with a story by Terry Dobson (1983) about an American Aikido student in Japan. We summarize the story in our own words with the addition of seven short quotations from the original dialogue. Readers can find the story it in its entirety by googling "Aikido in Action." A consideration of how words alone replace the need to use force sets the stage for understanding how to build an ethical community. A discussion follows of the role that family values play, the power of community projects, and the meaning of ethics in light of an evolving junior high community.

* * *

In the schoolyard, Dan insisted that he and his classmates had the skills to solve a problem among themselves without calling for an adult—which he worried would take up most of their valuable playtime. Maybe Dan had been influenced in his thinking about the power of his words by the story *Aikido in Action*, which Donna read to the junior high every year.

"Hey!!"

Earsplitting like a piercing whistle, but lilting and strangely joyous, as happens when we find something lost. It was so loud that everyone suddenly stood still. The train car was bound for the suburbs of Tokyo. An enraged drunk swung at a woman and her baby, spinning her into the laps of an elderly couple. The likely hero trained in aikido eight hours a day stood up.

Though an American whom the Japanese called a gaijin, a foreigner, he knew something must be done. He faced the drunk but waited for him to make the first move. Following the lofty teachings of aikido, he knew not to start a fight.

The antihero was spraying spittle, screaming "Gaijin," and gathering himself up for a rush at his new adversary. The gaijin had pursed his lips and blown him an insolent kiss. It was in this moment the loud and penetrating "hey" stopped them in their tracks.

Ignoring the American, a little old Japanese man dressed in a kimono looked up at the drunk and beamed, "What'cha been drinkin'?" "I've been drinkin' sake," the bully bellowed, "and it's none of your business!" "Oh, that's wonderful!" the old man responded, and with a slight movement of his hand he beckoned him to come closer. "C'mere and talk with me." And then, after a little more bellicosity that soon began softening, the old man proceeded to tell him a story of how he and his wife loved sake too. And how they would go out in the evening to watch the sunset, sitting on a wooden bench in a little garden, and drink their sake, rain or shine. To this he added how they needed to see how the persimmon tree was coping with the injuries it had suffered in the last winter ice storm. He then ventured, "And I'm sure you have a wonderful wife," and the despair was loosened. Sobbing, the bully said in the vernacular that his wife had died and that he had no home and no job, then added, "I'm so ashamed of myself."

At this point, Donna can't stop herself from crying too—making it difficult to read. She asks one of the children to finish the story, and then they discuss what can be learned from the tale. To begin with, she doesn't know whether the story really happened or not. The real lesson is figuring out how we find ways to make our voices powerful.

Building Community

Our voices are the building blocks of community, and they fit uniquely into understanding and practicing ethics. Were ethics a body of accepted knowledge transmitted as is from one generation to the next, the task would be different. Admittedly, this more fixed belief system is common in many cultures. But developing community ethics in our view is a collaborative social endeavor (Ryan and Bohlin 1999). We seek overlapping points of view that allow for living together agreeably. We bet on informed agreement where meaning is the expression of many voices—and careful listening.

In a classroom discussion, a compelling story like *Aikido in Action* can form the center of a search for common intellectual ground. The task is made easier because the emotional response is always quite similar. Discussion isn't meant to find one opinion. But the range of opinions together forms a narrative touched by a shared sense of authenticity. A really good book, a powerful short story, an essay about a common problem, a terrific poem, or a personal experience that touches many hearts can deepen cognitive knowledge, increase understanding, and widen possibilities for practical action.

Aikido and karate, like other martial arts, are learned as part of the development of a community spirit. The teachers decide what virtues to teach. It can be a very uplifting experience. When practicing karate, our grandson focuses on peace, friendship, and other responsibilities that make him a helpful member of his community.

A creative virtue of Aikido is the strategy of embracing negative energy and working to turn it around. There is an important element of defense, but the philosophy centers on a transformation that brings people together. Often this virtue is based on the power of words—not physical actions—using the same strategy.

In *Building Character in Schools* (1999), Kevin Ryan and Karen Bohlin write that building a group spirit is the essence of a "community of virtue." Building close relationships, caring enough to correct others, encouraging student ownership, and remembering the little things are all actions that support this development. For Ryan and Bohlin, ethics means more than getting along. It must embrace community service, bringing together enthusiasm and actions and all around aiming higher.

Whether in a martial art or the art of life, the community spirit harnesses strength—for the good, if we so choose.

Nuanced Thinking

The "word web" introduced in the last chapter can lead to more nuanced thinking about community ethics. In the center of a large poster, "ethics" is written in bold capital letters, leaving most of the poster board blank. The invitation is to create a "picture" of words allowing everyone (and even gently pushing some, if necessary) to make a contribution. The task can be accomplished with just two, but it is more interesting and fun when the ideas come from a group of young people. There is also room for a few ideas from the adults.

Kids are encouraged to pay attention to the contributions of others and to respond to all the ideas. Encouraging curiosity helps. Openness to new kinds of thinking signals success because it demonstrates responsiveness. From this work, the necessary effort for developing community ethics has begun—allowing a larger and more inclusive picture to emerge (Caldwell 2000; Mendieta and VanAntwerpen 2011; Ryan and Bohlin 1999).

On another day, there is time to write a short paragraph describing a personal experience: something about witnessing an ethical behavior, a quandary, an example of a good decision or a poor one. With these in hand and shared, there is an opportunity to think about how the word picture relates to these personal experiences. Does one of the ideas capture a story perfectly? Do several words establish a connection between the story and a concept? Can the children come up with a simple idea about why or how this connection exists? Does a practical guideline come to mind that might anticipate a conflict and serve as a tool to avoid problems before they occur? Maybe practical considerations are less important than finding children thinking and talking about ethics as if it were a common thing to do. Young people engaged in ethical thinking are proud of doing important work.

If an unresolved conflict comes up, this is an opportunity for the adult to facilitate a focused discussion (Horton and Freire 1990). A thorough discussion, with well-structured opportunities for talking and insistence on attentive listening, stimulates deeper discussion (Jackson, Boostrom, and Hansen 1993). Before the group settles on a practical resolution, a theoretical analysis must first focus on learning more about ethics in general—so often imagined outside the interests and skills of children this age (Damon 1988). When the people involved in the conflict are present, the discussion will be more meaningful and richer. Detailed listening can be structured so that each person's view is told separately. We recall how in the Japanese film *Rashomon* witnesses dramatically tell contrary stories of what occurred. It is useful to wonder how this happens.

Connecting experience and ideas leads to longer-range academic and artistic projects. Combining intellectual work with artistic expression is even more motivating. The interplay of intellectual and emotional thinking adds hues to a course of study. The picture of ethical thinking becomes more nuanced—and the practice of ethics more straightforward. Learning how to ask and answer the question, Is this ethical? is the underlying goal. Asking packs the strongest impact when the question arises at the moment when it is most needed. Different modes of exploration joined together embody learning, where it is transformed from a surface experience into a livelier one that touches a variety of relevant contexts. A good example is the illustration Shayma drew for "closed in" and contributed to the word web focused on bullying—a heart behind an iron grate.

The collaborative creation of knowledge forms bonds that are strengthened by accomplishments and opportunities to enjoy more options in children's everyday young lives. The benefits arise from a sense that acting in a more mature way does not limit behavior but indeed increases the degrees of freedom. This in no way means that a child is to be treated as an adult. Age-appropriate new options, however, are uncovered that add to young people's repertoires. There are new responsibilities, but because they are intrinsically related to possibilities, they are not likely to be a burden.

Text Box 5.1 The Religious and the Secular

Building Character in Schools by Kevin Ryan and Karen Bohlin (1999)
Making a Home for Faith by Elizabeth Caldwell (2000)
The Power of Religion in the Public Sphere edited by Eduardo Mendieta and Jonathan VanAntwerpen (2011)

Ryan and Bohlin offer a secular process for the collaborative creation of a community of virtue. Caldwell presents a religious curriculum for learning the values of faith. Even though we practice a separation of church and state in our public schools, there is significant overlap in every sphere of our lives. Choosing virtues to enhance the study of ethics is fraught with palpable tensions. "There are important moral truths that must be understood" (Ryan and Bohlin 1999, 38). But which ones?

There are many traditions from which to choose: religious, secular, and historical customs, as well as the wisdom that abounds in the older, the younger, and leaders of all stripes. Mendieta and VanAntwerpen bring attention to our "inhabiting a common world without universally shared absolutes or notions of transcendence of that worldliness. It's a problem that is set up by being in that predicament together" (2011, 109). They are referring to world politics, but this predicament faces every community from the biggest to the smallest. We can be sure of our own beliefs but not that everyone will join in our confidence.

Diversity needs to be honored. So must the problems that diversity brings forth. Hopelessness is an option, but it doesn't hold a candle to an ethical community spirit.

Family

What happens in school or with strangers on train cars can, at best, only make sense in connection with what is learned at home (Kagan and Lamb 1987; Kegan 1994). Conflict and collaborative ethical thinking begin with learning to talk. Parental use of the word "no" is ubiquitous and a harbinger for when children themselves will soon enough join in the choir. For parents, the message at first has to do with safety and boundaries. They are telling the child what is dangerous and what is permitted, given that adults too have wants and needs, for example, "It's time to go to sleep." And, without fanfare, it is not long before the message has to do with right and wrong. On the other side of the coin, at around age two, children also become adept at using the word "no." Here begin confrontations that might entail right versus right.

The learning that children do elsewhere builds on how a family copes with its own ethics, even as a matter of unlearning (Kegan 1994). Growing older, children become more articulate, and their reasoning becomes more complex. Arguments, the stuff of human disagreements, are natural in the course of every family's development, and how they are navigated and negotiated becomes the model for coping imprinted on a young person. How parents manage their adult responsibilities is a critical element of this model; a more significant factor lies in how all members of the family go about their daily lives functioning together. Personally, all that we did and do as teachers was integral to the education of our own children. But what we learned from family life was miles more complicated than what we experienced as teachers. Raising children even turns scary when the time comes to let go. The best learning happened when we as a family worked problems out together.

For us, contrary to common opinion that children are not sufficiently developed to deal with ethical issues, we consider children fully human (Wall 2010). The very real differences are a matter of degree, not kind. Our children were adequate to the task of contributing a valuable share to the dialogue. Even before they could talk, there at times occurred a kind of two-sided communication that had elements of bargaining. Once they were talking, we continued, and this is what we did to negotiate our daily lives together. Unlike in classrooms, the vicissitudes of life in many ways controlled how much we could do in a rationally intentional manner. So much and so often, we were improvising. But we trusted the process and welcomed how

---

Text Box 5.2 Following the Rules and Becoming a Social Being

The Moral Child by William Damon (1988)
In Over Our Heads by Robert Kegan (1994)

Consider four of Damon's precepts and Kegan's three principles. Reconcile the precepts and the principles.

1. "Permissiveness and restrictiveness ... do not have a direct or predictable influence on children's morality" (Damon 1988, 57).
2. "Introducing children to the social order means more than just getting them to obey certain rules. It also means inculcating in children an abiding respect for the social order itself" (Damon 1988, 52).
3. "The closely affectionate relationship that most parents enjoy with their children normally induces an inclination to cooperate" (Damon 1988, 52).
4. "In this sense, secure children obey voluntarily from 'within' the relationship, rather than out of coercion or fear" (Damon 1988, 52).

Three principles: Early on, "children's attachment to the momentary, the immediate, and the atomistic makes ... their feelings impulsive and fluid, their social-relating egocentric" (Kegan 1994, 29). Between the ages of seven and ten, "children's capacity to organize things, others, and the self as possessors of elements or properties ... [enables them] to grant to themselves and others a separate mind and a distinct point of view" (Kegan 1994, 29). With adolescents, we expect abstract thinking; "their feelings [are] a matter of inner states and self-reflexive emotion" and "their social-relating [is] capable of loyalty and devotion to a community of people or ideas larger than the self" (Kegan 1994, 29, 32).

---

it evolved. For better or worse, our children's knowledge and understanding of ethics began with our family and all that we as a family engaged in with others.

The talking, the listening, and the process were the tools we used to build our community of four. The dimensions of our experiences are clearer in retrospect than they were then; still, we managed and succeeded in important ways to grow together in responsiveness to each other. As parents, we worked at expanding our repertoire of positive responses to their growing range of behaviors from the time they were infants. In our efforts to ask for their responsiveness to our needs and requests, no doubt we couldn't always be positive. No surprise. But between the two of us, we rarely lost sight of a reality based on creative interactions among the four of us—knowing that this was the most rewarding course of action. Children (and adults) normally expect moral teachings from an unresponsive top-down position. And adults do have knowledge that needs to be honored. Still, there is an advantage to making room for mutual responsiveness in social learning of all kinds. The likelihood of adherence to social and ethical behaviors is improved, and there is an even greater chance that other opportunities for living collaboratively together will appear spontaneously.

Interpersonal Relationships

The development of interpersonal relationships obviously happens more fruitfully under positive conditions. It would seem so, but normative patterns are usually otherwise. It is normal to circle the wagons and clarify personal wants, and this is considered a reasonable approach. It doesn't help that ethics leans toward making laws and enforcing them. Important attention to the contexts in which family conflicts exist is then largely missing. But expanding the domain of family dynamics reveals that there is knowledge to be gained from those younger than we that can come into play. Children's self-expression has great potential for surprising and enlightening us. There is much for us to learn in these behaviors that can deepen our understanding of how vital relationships are created. This knowledge and top-down knowledge do not trump each other. Children present us with fruitful opportunities for creating a mutually nurturing living space for all (Damon 1988).

Children and adults can, at the same time, learn to be more creative. Building community and understanding ethics come together as one integrated task. To begin, as parents we know that some aspects of raising children have little room for negotiation. Legitimate top-down boundaries need to be in place. We also know that our children's bottom-up otherness demands attention and nurturance. These personal viewpoints meet in a generative relational space. It uncovers new common ground. Loving relationships can form based on satisfying work and play. There will be a share of difficult times, but more often, we can expect a sense of success and joy.

We do well to believe that we all have the ability to change how we see each other. The interpretations we hold of others are in our power to rethink and refeel—at any time. Also, we can constantly recreate our inner narratives about our own lives. The goal is to move toward an ever-expanding field in which to meet and live with the narratives and interpretations in their formation of new common ground (Blum 1987; Kegan 1994; Wall 2010).

Certainly, when our children were young, they had no consciousness of this. But then again, neither did we. We did know that we had to grow together. As adults, we continuously had to learn more about ourselves. This fostered getting along in growthful ways in our lives together. In general, this kind of growth leads to more satisfying community experiences and the foundations of ethical thinking. We drain the joys of living by working too hard on getting our own way. Finding paths that unify us as a joyful team is better. The full meaning of and responsibility for responsiveness to each other become clearer. The ethical life we see then is a continuous expansion of self.

In 1987, L. Blum suggested that "responsiveness should be seen as a moral phenomenon ... and in children is one developmental forerunner of the adult's moral virtues of compassion, kindness, helpfulness, sympathy, and the like" (319). For the more modern reader, John Wall, in *Ethics in Light of Childhood*, enlarges the meaning of this concept: "What children and adults gain morally from families is a close circle of interdependent relations in which to create lasting stories and shared responsibilities. [The] practice of ethical thinking is not just applying ordered principles, expressing autonomous freedom, [or] progressing in social reason, but forging expanding horizons ... [an] other-responsive art that strives against narrowness and complacency to imagine an always more inclusive humanity" (2010, 180).

Thinking like this is to dream and to know that reality is stimulated by dreams. "Decide for yourself what dreams can come true" (advice from a fortune cookie that Jerry opened a long time ago). Particularly in the family, but also in every community, we each have personal evidence of this expansion. Amid a sea of stress, we must focus on the practical. Out of the particulars, we find a common ethics that helps us cope and live together. Theory evolves into practice—and what counts most is the work we do from our own hearts with others.

Community Projects

In school, at home, and in the local community, collaborative projects are a means to express ethical behavior that broadens learning—in action and in conceptual understanding. The work is proactive as it helps to shift a social environment away from dysfunctional behavior.

Joining young people together to undertake service projects of all kinds sets a positive social mood while it teaches positive values. The strategy is to aim toward doable tasks that are likely to satisfy a wide range of interests as a part of discovering the rewards of hard work in something other than profiting only oneself. This work is important, too, because it includes a valuable sense of accomplishment. It is no different than for people of any age. The feelings join with the increase of knowledge, and together these experiences serve as bedrock for confidence and hope in the possibility of leading an ethical life (Lewis 2008).

Some projects touch on ethics indirectly. With Donna as the teacher for many years and always with the help of others, and now Lisa Pack, our sister-in-law, the Project Learn School now publishes the *PL Paper* as part of a journalism course. Issued four to six issues a year, the paper reports on topics related to the school program and the people who are part of making it happen, as well as a variety of local community news. One benefit is an understanding of the broad context within which the Project Learn School functions—for the children and for the parents. The traditions that reporters uphold are introduced to the children. They are taught the meaning of free speech, just as they are required to meet the standards of quality reporting. They learn to take the time to report information accurately and to be certain that quotes really reflect what a person said. The reporters are pushed to include opposing opinions. One year, for example, it turned out that not all the children in the school enjoyed the Halloween party. Some of the younger ones indeed felt very frightened by the spook house constructed by the junior high. Donna required the coreporters to ask some of these children to express their opinions in addition to presenting the positive reactions of the majority of the students. Recently, news of the ethics course we were teaching appeared on the front page.

Ethics in Light of a Junior High Community

Ethics is about people getting along. This is what we say to our students. In the long run, the aim is to achieve a more complex understanding of interdependency. It is possible, from this starting point, with the reading of compelling books and writing about personal experience, to introduce more complexity over time. Tough-minded discussions and activities within a small community of friends, fellow

VOLUME XXX ISSUE 3

PLS Paper
A student newspaper
6525 Germantown Ave., Philadelphia, PA 19119

PROJECT
LEARN
SCHOOL
COOPERATIVE • PROGRESSIVE • EDUCATION

An Interview from the Ethics Class

Community Ethics

By Irene Lobron

Marvin Hite, who has a MSS from Bryn Mawr College, is a retired Drug and Alcohol Counselor from the Philadelphia Prison System. He came to talk to a group of Junior High Students at Project Learn School about community ethics for the ethics class that Jerry Allender has been teaching. He brought with him three home school students who he teaches ethics to. During his visit at school, I got a chance to interview him about his experience with community ethics.

Irene: What does a community need in order to be ethical?

Marvin: I believe that an ethical community needs a set of rules that are followed without being policed by others. People should be able to do what is right without constantly being reminded.

Irene: How did you get started with community ethics?

Marvin: I got a job as a drug and alcohol counselor in the Philadelphia Prison System. People do unethical things because of the impact drugs can have on them. I trained myself so that I could handle more problems.

Irene: What ethics do people need to work well in a community?

Marvin: They need to have education about ethics, and they need to be morally right in order for a community to function right.

Irene: What interests you about community ethics?

Marvin: I really hate to see people get bullied or taken ad-

vantage of, and I want to make sure people get treated right.

Irene: What do you think an individual can do to help in his or her community?

Marvin: They have to keep a flow of information to the powers. . .the powers being the police. . .about any situation that is not morally sound or ethically proper.

Irene: What is the outcome when somebody does not contribute to his or her community?

Marvin: Problems and chaos. A little problem becomes a bigger problem, and a bigger problem becomes destruction. So basically problems occur.

Irene Lobron's Response:

I had never really thought about community ethics before I go a chance to talk with Marvin Hite. But after I talked to him, I think I now am more conscious of what it is and how it works. It was very interesting for me to hear about his experience with it. I hope one day everybody will have a good understanding of what you need in order to have a well functioning community and have a good environment to live in.

Marvin Hite

Ethics Exhibit Emerges at High Point Cafe

By Isaac Adlowitz

Four Ethics teachers: Tal Ben-Yaacov, Jerry Allender, Jason Huber, and Marvin Hite, outside the High Point Cafe.

Once again ethics was taught at PLS, but this time Jason's Group took it. Last semester Liz and Liam's group took ethics as the guinea pigs for the Junior High. This semester it was PLS Ethics II, and there were three teachers who taught ethics to Jason's Group. They were Jerry Allender, Jason Huber, and Tal Ben-Yaacov. Also, during the semester there were lots of special guests helping teach different lessons. The written work and art work from both classes resulted in an Ethics Exhibit, which was put up at the High Pint Café on Carpenter Avenue from April 2 to April 14.

In PLS Ethics II, there was one teacher who taught both Jason and Liz and Liam's Groups. That teacher is Jerry Allender. He talked about teaching ethics at PLS. "I was 73 years old and I was

Continued on page 5

Visit Project Learn Paper's Blog at:
plspaper.blogspot.com

Photo 5.1 The *PL Paper*

students, troublemakers, and leaders can change behaviors. The power of the community is best understood in action, particularly with adolescents—who are inclined to act strongly for ill or for good (Kegan 1994; Wall 2010).

The study of ethics can be an integral part of building a community of young people. Learning concepts related to laws, rules, agreements, and compassion; struggling with an understanding of right versus right; and learning how to converse using a vocabulary that includes these concepts make up the important academic half of the work—irrespective of whether it is taking place in school or not (Kidder 1995, 2005). The other half is the necessary practice it takes to learn how to get along in the already complex life of a junior high community. This needs to be experienced as a daily exercise where failure and success are expected and encouraged in the ongoing life of the community. We need to take note of John Dewey's (1938) concern for participating in the experience of our education.

These two aspects of learning, the theoretical and the practical, provide each other with a unique kind of feedback, and this is yet another dimension of the knowledge to be gained. A space is created that allows for someone to say, "I don't think what you are doing is ethical." Given an understanding that ethics are messy, saying this initiates, rather than concludes, a conversation. In this kind of environment, the humanistic elements of education embody the best strategy for collaborative success (Allender and Allender 2008). They facilitate coping with messiness that is necessarily operating (Coady 2008). By "building a democratic community," junior high students realize "a radical approach to moral education" (Power 2002).

Bringing together the acquisition and the practice of knowledge becomes a context within which breakdowns in the social fabric can manifest themselves as opportunities for more learning, rather than as showstoppers that interfere with the ongoing flow of productive group experience. In place of calling upon an adult to act like a cop when something bad is happening—for example, when we see bullying—a group awareness emerges that this is everybody's business and that everyone has responsibility for searching together for solutions (Kristol 2002).

The scope of concerns goes far beyond problems of bullying. Some offenses disrespect the work of other children or break school rules, for instance, against cheating and plagiarizing. Some infringe on another's property. Sometimes the problems involve broken agreements made between children or between adults or both. And of course, unlawful and even criminal behaviors are possible. Given the gift of human creativity, there is no end to the list. We can hope that working with a broad strategy will help children avoid problems before they occur. Confrontation is an expected process; our strategy is to engage many levels of learning.

CHAPTER 6

WORK ETHIC

Poor-quality work normally does not qualify as unethical. Cheating and plagiarism qualify, because they are dishonest. However, when students routinely do not pay diligent attention to their schoolwork and exhibit poor workmanship, it is fair to judge them. For teachers, this can elicit an inner cry of despair that often results in railing that threatens students with dire consequences. We can reasonably say this kind of workmanship reflects the lack of a work ethic.

To the best of our ability, we aim toward a kinder approach to the problem, but one that insists that each student truly achieve academic quality that demonstrates his or her best abilities. Toward this end, we discuss the meaning of commitment, the expression of schoolwork with realistic goals, and some notions of what constitutes acceptable achievement. Individual efforts have an important place in this process. However, given the value we place on collaborative work, we also discuss the value of work achieved by groups. Small groups offer children opportunities to contribute their special skills in ways that leave no one looking like a slacker.

The chapter includes an example of an entire class project that leads to an exciting expression of work ethic for all of the students, providing a model for the development of their own work ethic. And possibilities for acquiring other guiding visions of hard work are tapped in what can be learned from children's literature. Overall, we see limitations and potential; more relevantly, we cover lots of middle ground.

A good place to begin an exploration of work ethic is to ask about our personal commitment to do what we say we will. We ourselves must believe that the work will get done, and it is important to communicate this to others with our attitude. It helps even more when others believe that we will be responsible for doing a job we said we would do.

Text Box 6.1 Teamwork and Me

TOGETHER WE WIN

Photo 6.1   Photo 6.2

The Great War and World War II. "We Can Do It, Together We Win." So many people were willing to work hard and work together. There was a great show of the spirit it takes to accomplish what one wants and what the country needed. Good for them, and good for us!

It is a shame that this wonderful energy was organized around two horrific wars. A story is told, though, about what can be accomplished in every other sphere of life. Alone, competing, or cooperating, we can create something or make something happen.

Levels of commitment are not the same for a person from task to task.

What kind of work is involved? Is the task being done alone? Are others involved? Who will judge the quality of the job done? Others? Oneself? What are strategies for encouraging children to match their promises with their actions? What kinds of scaffolding can be used to help children to learn such a skill? How and where does positive feedback fit into the picture? Answers to these questions and others like them lead to courses of action that are likely to influence the development of commitment. Identifying the particular meaning of commitment, by working with these questions, is a step toward understanding a child's potential for making and keeping commitments.

Having a reputation for a good work ethic lets others know that we are someone who is willing to work hard. This reputation is created by a track record that shows others that it has been earned. But equally important is the inner message that accompanies the building of this track record. Seeing oneself as a hard worker bolsters the image. Together, the inner voice and the story held by others create a feedback loop that serves to strengthen the work ethic as it is growing. We must recognize that there are times when anyone can have difficulties honoring commitments. Admitting this is a powerful source of empathy. From this vantage, the reputation earned is not easily lost. Notice that children and adults are not so different at times. We can interpret the efforts of young people in a positive light, despite their failings, as we help them build, maybe unsteadily at times, a work ethic.

The hard work accomplished supplies the elements of a story that we can tell about ourselves and the one told by others. In the beginning, a child may exert only a small amount of energy. Beginnings come in all shapes and sizes. The initial energy might not be recognized, and the message the child receives is that the effort was not worthwhile. The story can be biased in the child's favor so that this initial positive experience can be built on as a path to a stronger work ethic. Still, it's important for adults not to exaggerate the value of any effort, small or big—making it seem enough when it really isn't. How adults interpret children's work is important and a tough call. The goal is to encourage high-quality work as judged by the self and others. Beginning with commitment as the starting point exposes the roots of a work ethic. What happens informs us about what has been accomplished and what more needs to be done.

On the surface, it would seem that developing a work ethic is about an internalized sense of responsibility; yet the discussion is far more about social interaction. No doubt, the hard work of personal learning and change is an important part of what has to happen. Such efforts confront and challenge conflicting desires. Everyone knows the struggle between wanting to read or relax in other ways when something else needs to be done. Children face this struggle particularly when they have not fully internalized their responsibility to a task. These struggles are less social when related to internal processes.

To learn about commitment, however, we have found that children must be engaged socially in work accomplished by a well-knit group that results in a mix of challenging academic learning and satisfying personal expression. Successful group work entails important and memorable experience that cements academic knowledge and practical experience as one. Teamwork garners rewards that cannot accrue when one works alone. Many good feelings derive from what one, as an individual, accomplishes, whether it has to do with gaining knowledge, making a product, or helping someone in need. But the efforts of people working as a team have a special value for children becoming adolescents. Teamwork introduces them to a sense of community at a new level that fits well with their growing awareness. Meeting the need to join with others their age can make commitment doubly satisfying.

Small Groups in Elementary School

There is no way to teach work ethics except by doing. Early in her teaching career starting in 1957, before Donna met Jerry, she had children work together in small groups to learn and then teach about a subject. She was teaching third grade at that time. One of her favorite projects was learning about simple machines that were then a standard part of the third-grade science curriculum. She divided the children into small groups, each of which was responsible for learning about one of the simple machines: levers, pulleys, inclined planes, wheels and axles, wedges, and screws.

Each group had to develop a demonstration model of its machine that the other children could operate. Group members had to present what they learned on a poster board with a story about the machine and drawings illustrating its actions. Finally, as experts on their particular machine, they had to prepare a presentation for the rest of the class, acting in her place as the teacher. The more proficient students supported those who had difficulty reading. Those who were writers helped their classmates learn better writing skills, and everyone helped with the presentation. To the child, they worked as hard as Donna, who, after all the presentations had been made, suggested that they might enjoy making their presentations to another class. It was decided to invite one of the second-grade classes into the room and to teach its students about simple machines.

Each child felt his or her accomplishment when the project was completed. There is no question that it took a lot of Donna's time to make all this happen, what with teacher guidance, support, and oft-repeated directions. Although it entailed far more work than teaching by the book, the outcome not only produced knowledge but helped create a work ethic that beautifully connected the children intellectually and emotionally to the class sense of community.

PLS Paper
A student newspaper
6525 Germantown Ave., Philadelphia, PA 19119

Interview from the Ethics Class

Work Ethics

By Gabe Beresin

As you may or may not have heard, the Junior High students at Project Learn School are studying ethics. This is an interview with Liam Gallagher, the science teacher, about work ethics. This will explain Liam's thoughts about having a work ethic and what it means to him. Work ethic is very important to Liam and that is why I chose to interview him.

Gabe: Why is work ethics so important to you?

Liam: I believe that a person's work ethic reveals a lot about that person's character. A person who takes pride in her or his work is a person that I want to be around and work with. I don't care for people who feel they are entitled to something without working for it.

Gabe: Do you think of yourself as having a good work ethic? Why?

Liam: In general, I feel that I have a good work ethic. I've successfully completed high school, college and graduate school. If I didn't

have a good work ethic, I'm not sure I would have made it through. I also think I have a good work ethic, because I've received positive feedback from my professors and employers throughout the years. If I'm proud of what I do, I consider it a job well done.

Gabe: What do you expect from a person with a good work ethic?

Liam: I expect to see a certain degree of pride and excitement from that person. A person with a good work ethic is often excited to share their work with others and knows when it is time to get down to business.

Gabe: What is your definition of work ethic?

Liam: Every person will have his unique work ethic, so it is hard to put an exact definition to it. I would describe work ethic as how a person approaches an assignment, a task or project. There can be negative work ethics such as late, lazy, or uninspired, and there can be positive work ethics such as punctual, prideful and thorough.

Gabe: Do you think that work ethic is

something you work on and it gets better as you work, or do you think it is something that comes easily?

Liam: Another great question. I feel that it is something you work on as you get older. I am sure some people find it easier that others, but everyone can develop a good work ethic. I know plenty of people who were never great students, but they worked harder than anyone I know. They have developed a great sense of integrity and humility that comes along with the fact that they earned everything they have achieved.

Gabe Beresin's Response:

Integrity, which means feeling good about yourself in an honest way, is balanced by humility. Liam is a person who is not afraid to talk about work ethic. Most people are afraid that if they are too full of themselves, then they might sound egotistical. If they are not confident, no one wants to talk to them. Liam models great balance between integrity and humility, and I admire that he is brave enough to talk about it.

Photo 6.3 Student Reporter

Donna Shares Stories of Teaching and Growing Up

Going Places

Junior high students, some student teachers, and I wrote *Going Places* as a guide to Philadelphia for other teenagers to use when they visited the city during the bicentennial. The idea for doing the book evolved from a discussion we had about what we would study during group time, a portion of the school day set aside for students to work together on a learning project. There were no limits as to what could be studied, but there were clear requirements for engaging in the process. The students had to agree by consensus on what they wanted to learn. We had to find an interesting angle that worked for each person and enabled me to ensure a deep engagement in the project for all of us. Of course many topics were proposed, and for each I listed the kind of work to which we would need to commit.

"Donna, I think we should study baseball." "Okay," I said. "Remember, though, any project we do has to include study from different points of view." We discussed what we might do: Maybe we would learn about some of the physics of ball playing, the mathematics behind the many statistics that come with the sport, and the social science that helps to explain its role in society. Maybe we would study how major league baseball became integrated. There could be artwork showing how baseball is played, perhaps with some humorous depictions of ball players. The plan would lead to written presentations. Then, we would have to think about presenting our work to the other children in the school, the parents, and perhaps to children in other schools, as well as forming teams and playing some ball. The youngster with the baseball idea really just wanted to play baseball during group time. He withdrew his suggestion!

After several discussions, someone suggested visiting and writing about places in Philadelphia. The idea was to take trips to all the different city locations of interest to teenagers: museums, parks, video arcades, and great hamburger joints. There was a groundswell of enthusiasm. I let the students know that we had to have a reason for visiting all these fun places. We broke into small groups and talked about what the purpose might be, and after much deliberation, we decided that we would publish a book for other kids to use. And then we realized that we could market the book to bookstores in the city.

We outlined all the efforts necessary to produce such a book. Everyone was clear about wanting to travel around the city, and I was clear that there would be very strict plans to make sure this was done safely. For publishing the book, we divided up the task areas: written descriptions, artwork, photography, maps, bus directions, and evaluations of each place visited.

It became clear to all of us that this project depended on every person doing what he or she agreed to do. Everyone had to do some research, some writing, and some artwork or other task not covered as well. Without each person's efforts, we would not have had a book to sell. And sell a book we did—to many of the bookstores in Philadelphia.

Importantly, in this project, each student knew her or his work was critical to its success. I made sure that no one did anyone else's work to assure the success of the project and, more significantly, that everyone experienced a sense of authentic achievement. Each person had to come through or there would be no book. Each person had to demonstrate an effective work ethic. We sold over three hundred copies and had money left over for a junior high trip.

An Infinite World of Possibilities

For many teachers, parents, and others who engage with adolescents, such an extensive project is not usually possible. But many less complicated activities require individuals to work hard for the goals of a group. When children join with an adult to build a tree house, they need both intellectual and practical knowledge. The house will not get built if they do not have plans and measurements or if they are distracted and run off to play soccer. They must focus their energy on the task and the learning required to get the job done.

There are so many other possibilities for projects for interested adults to undertake with a small group of young people. When I was growing

---

Text Box 6.2 Protestant Work Ethic

Photo 6.4

The Protestant Ethic and the Spirit of Capitalism by Max Weber (1930)
The Emergence of Morality in Young Children by Jerome Kagan and Sharon Lamb (1987)

Grant Wood painted *American Gothic*, hanging in the Art Institute of Chicago, in 1930, the same year that Talcott Parsons translated Weber's book into English—an appealing coincidence. The painting is commonly interpreted as a representation of the Puritan work ethic, an idea that harkens back to the Reformation of Martin Luther five centuries ago. This work ethic from the Renaissance with its grand meanings and egregious faults stays with us to this day.

Kagan and Lamb describe how it need not be explicitly preached but can instead be implicitly communicated in planned educational environments: "The work ethic assumes concrete form as 'Keep busy, be purposeful' ... and 'Do as much as you can without teacher assistance'" (1987, 142).

up, the kids in my neighborhood, from the five-year-olds to the high school students, joined together to build two snow forts in the park across the street from our homes. In the 1940s in Minneapolis, such forts would last the entire winter. They had to be built carefully to endure the many snowball fights that ensued. Older children taught the younger ones how thick the base squares had to be, how big the fort should be, and where and how to build the doors, the windows, and the peepholes. Everyone worked hard on both forts, for we all knew that the teams would be different each time there was a fight. After the fights, we all went to my house for hot chocolate, because everyone knew my mother made the best cookies. I do not know when the ritual of building forts began, but I do know we all learned about working together.

Taran Wanderer

Lloyd Alexander wrote great stories for young adults, and one of Jerry's and my favorites is *Taran Wanderer*, the fourth of five in the *Chronicles of Prydain* series based on Celtic myth. In this exciting and stunning writing, ethical problems surface on every other page. And *Taran Wanderer* is all about a work ethic.

Every time I read the book, I cry and learn something new about relationships from a small group of very different people who are traveling together—and other people who are often helpful, some who are dangerous to them, and a few whose mystery unfolds in surprising ways. But this book teaches especially about what it means to have a clear sense of responsibility toward work.

Besides assuming responsibility to the community, Taran engages in an individual quest for knowledge, just as we want our students to do in their studies. As Taran wanders a mythical ancient Welsh countryside looking for the kind of work that will satisfy his destiny, he encounters people who are models from which all of us can learn. We learn of his disappointments, as well as his joys, in meeting the artisans with whom he works for a time as an apprentice, including a weaver, a blacksmith, and a potter. The book provides a rich landscape for thinking about the meaning of work and combines high adventure with philosophy that challenges the growth of self—particularly for Taran, who had previously been simply an assistant pig keeper. The book draws students in and warrants some hard thinking by adolescents either at home or in school. It can be read, too, in a snow fort after a fight with friends over cups of hot chocolate.

Text Box 6.3 Taran, an Assistant Pig Keeper's Quest

Building Character in Schools by Kevin Ryan and Karen Bohlin (1999)
Taran Wanderer by Lloyd Alexander (1967)

"Experience is one of our greatest teachers. In the same way that competence in one's field is achieved with time and experience, moral maturity comes with experience. Character ... is not developed just by learning words such as kindness and honesty. It involves our whole life—what we think, and do, and why" (Ryan and Bohlin 1999, 145–146). Toward this end, Ryan and Bohlin have written about practical ways to bring moral instruction to life that include good ideas, action strategies, and sample curricula

In *Taran Wanderer*, the assistant pig keeper, at the end of his quest, peers into the magical Mirror of Llunet to discover that it is nothing more than a small, shallow pool of water showing his own reflection. "You saw nothing then?" Annlaw, the potter, queries. "I learned what I sought to learn," Taran replied. "In the time I watched, I saw strength—and frailty. Pride and vanity, courage and fear. Of wisdom, a little. Of folly, much. Of intentions, many good ones; but many more left undone. In this alas, I saw myself a man like any other" (Alexander 1967, 270).

Years have passed as he nears the close of his adventures; Taran has grown from a boy into a man.

Are They Wretched Adolescents?

It can happen that we will feel hopeless. Living and working with these children becoming adolescents might appear an endless and often futile struggle to instill a sense of responsibility. However true this might often be, our frustration is stimulated by a problematic stereotype. Stereotypes are bad habits. More truthfully, the behavior of children this age covers a wide range of responses—from resistance to dedication—to the value of work and getting it done. Learning responsibility is not a linear process, and it cannot be accomplished without some trial and error, error being the key word. Guidance must take into account how commonplace frustration will be for children and adults.

We can find strength in knowing that the negative and the positive are integral parts of a relationship that feeds healthy growth and development. However much it might seem possible to mold children into responsible members of their communities, the likely response to this approach is stronger resistance. Becoming an adolescent means finding an identity that distinguishes oneself from others, a predominant planetary concern of young people. In our minds, a work ethic grows out of an expansion of self-expression and connections with others. This is a world that moves cyclically through phases of excitement and frustration over and over again. All the while, creativity is released that heightens the probability that connections will appear.

The goal is to make connections with others that encourage compatible expressions of self. These are not necessarily conscious actions for young people, but surely intentionality is a smart strategy for the grown-ups with whom they spend appreciable time interacting. The emphasis has to be on building relationships where expression of self results in workable actions for all. A productive cycle is one that allows everyone enough slack to move around in closeness, openness, and connectedness. Being closed protects the growth of self; being open allows matching energetic moments to occur. These are the times and places where personal wants and those of others luckily overlap enough to be connected in a lively relationship.

The doing of work is archetypal, and a work ethic is best grounded in the deep feelings attached to the archetypes. Real passion for work is not based on ideas that justify its importance. Releasing the passion for a job to be done comes with the expansion of self and creativity that make successful completion of the work more likely. Once again, the issues involved are common to children and adults. Both encounter

---

Text Box 6.4 Effort Offered, Effort Discouraged

E Is for Ethics by Ian James Corlett (2009)

"Elliot and Lucy weren't prepared for Dad raining on their parade" (75).

In short, summarized and paraphrased from pages 73–75, this is what happened:

> Prepared to spend a chunk of their day cleaning up the mess left by a festival the day before in the park across the street from their house, they were psyched. As their dad left for work that morning, he made things difficult. He said that the job was too big, and they had to call the park district and find other kids to help. Their grandpa had called them good citizens for offering their efforts. "I'm not sure I even want to be a citizen now," grumbled Lucy (74).

How would you end this story?*

"You may be disappointed if you fail, but doomed if you don't try" (words spoken by Beverly Sills—an opera singer from the twentieth century, with a beautiful voice, a clearly serious mind, who was also very funny at times).

* In the story, it all works out, but it could have easily gone another way.

difficulties that resist engagement of a strong work ethic. Unethical action is not more prominent among the young or the old.

As leaders, we will stumble at times, even on our way to grand successes. We can help young people to bring to their work the fullness of a competent and effective well-directed passion. We can strengthen our resolve by keeping in mind that this passion is universally available to children of all ages. When it is engaged, children growing through their young years grab onto their projects with lively energy—an energy that allows for learning and dedication to what they have chosen to be of significance. This part of work is not new to those now becoming adolescents. What is new is the growing ability to engage in learning, projects, and relationships that nurture both themselves and the community.

CHAPTER 7

GLOBAL CONCERNS

It is amazing how Rick Riordan, a popular prolific writer, can draw children into stories that involve Greek and Roman myth, their gods and goddesses, and modern global ethical problems to boot. In *The Lightning Thief* (2005, 190), Percy Jackson, a kid living in the modern world, is talking with Grover, a satyr who continues to exist in this same world:

> "But you still want to go," I said amazed. "I mean, you really think that you'll be the one to find Pan?"
>
> "I really have to believe that, Percy. Every searcher does. It's the only thing that keeps us from despair when we look at what humans have done to the world. I have to believe Pan can still be awakened."

Many communities and schools sponsor programs that address worldwide problems; some even invite worldwide participation. Our ever-developing technological and informational means of communication put teens in a position to initiate or join these projects. Young people's involvement in conserving the planet's resources, protecting human rights, addressing poverty, advocating for peace, and working toward righting other sorts of malaise is newsworthy. As these activities become commonplace, with and without conscious effort, new ethical considerations emerge.

Some of the discussion deals with the same issues we have touched on already. Learning what it takes for people to get along persists, but now in new, larger contexts. There are still conversations that focus on community building—on how our small groups can educate themselves about conflicts and successful developments that are taking place outside the school community. There are opportunities to become engaged face-to-face through activities with other communities. And today, with the Internet widely available to so many, the connections provide us with information and virtual communities with children and adults far afield.

Four topics are interwoven in the pages of this chapter: (1) shifting awarenesses that deepen our knowledge of everyday ethics, (2) reader activities that enliven the text, (3) media for involving different kinds of communicating, and (4) travel to places near and far.

Global goals would seem to require global participation. On the other hand, local service is certainly where we begin. Sometimes our actions do join with others afar—in the same town, another county, other states, and other countries—to have a truly global impact. However, the impact can be simply in one's own backyard, though accompanied by an awareness of the needs of people farther afield. It can all prove to be enough, but, for sure, the action begins locally. Out of this work come the possibilities for generating an expanded focus. Unexplored mysteries accompany the enlarged effort that goes beyond the scope of our relatively small and limited daily community. There is potential for exciting, challenging, and sometimes bewildering confrontations with what behaving ethically means.

The Teen Guide to Global Action by Barbara A. Lewis (2008) gives teachers enough information to plan a detailed curriculum. Lewis covers topics that include human rights, hunger and homelessness, health and safety, education, environment and conservation, youth representation, and peace and friendship—easily adaptable into daily plans for engaging students in relevant activities. A year later, Lewis (2009) published five hundred more activities "for young people who want to make a difference."

Subtitled *How to Connect with Others (Near and Far) to Create Social Change*, Lewis's *Teen Guide* is a compendium of practical ideas, stories of experience, advice on planning, strategies for research, myriad websites, and organizations to contact. All told, she shares hundreds of websites to explore. The word "global" refers to an expansion of local action from the family, to the school, community, city, state, and nation, to the planet itself. Every move outward from the center broadens the impact. Our minds are opened to a larger and larger context. In these actions, we initiate actions that embrace others in our circle of concern. We understand ethics not as restriction but as a grand process of inclusion.

Question: How much junk was left on the moon? The *Teen Guide* doesn't deal with littering space with dead satellites and tools accidently dropped during repairs. Backpackers know you are supposed to take out what you bring in. Search the Internet. It is easy to find the answer.

Knowing Strangers

Thinking about others who live on this planet as strangers we want to get to know, understand, learn from, and help is a worthy goal. It is valuable too to consider how our local community is a part of this global make up. We can look at ourselves from a perspective of how others might be viewing us—much like an anthropologist studying her or his own culture. An array of needs and values fills the world we live in. If we encourage this consciousness to unfold, it becomes a wondrous study and experience for learning.

This is the soup of ethical messiness in which we live. School, home, and the other places where young people move about are important elements, providing a large measure of safety and surety about what is happening and what is expected of them in their lives. The goals of education have to be understandable in part. There should a fair measure of dependable answers. But equally, it is time to confront the ambiguities that reality presents. In the zone of global concerns, the tensions between values are exacerbated—and yet, we stand to learn the most from these tensions.

We hold many assumptions that make it easier to navigate our everyday world with reasonable levels of stress. As we encourage young people to ponder more serious elements and to challenge some of these assumptions, it is essential to keep a sense of humor—if for no other reason than to offset peering into and confronting a world of seemingly intractable problems. There is a personal challenge, and there is a collective challenge. All learning by definition confronts the unknown. The study of ethics has more of this than usual—for all ages.

To address global concerns fully, some of the learning will truly be upsetting. One story stays in our hearts. It humbles us and any other teacher of ethics who is looking for the right things to say.

> Project Learn students at this age study the Holocaust. A touching moment was the time when a child said to her teacher, "Lisa," paused, then asked, "They didn't really do this to people, did they?"

There was no humor to soften the blow. What can one honestly say? The answer was yes. There are easier topics to teach, and we start now with these.

The Spinning Globe

Try this activity for real or in your mind. On a globe, find where you live. Describe your life. What it is like to live here. How do you and others get what you need? Where do you get food? How is your home? Not too cold or too hot? Does it protect you from bad weather?

Describe what you do during the day. Ask others what they have to say about living here. Try to build a consensus. Pay attention to noteworthy differences of opinion.

Now, spin the globe with your eyes shut. When it stops, put a finger down and see where you have landed. Describe this place to the best of your ability. Use your imagination if necessary. Ask for help from others. The discussion is likely to reveal transparent differences. Yet much can be the same.

List all that you think people need to live a fairly happy and meaningful life. Include thoughts about work, play, family, friends, food, shelter, and other things that you want to consider. Think about the people to whom you are related. List a lot of them. What are some of the helpful things that you do for these people?

Working with others, make a huge drawing that charts and relates these people to each other. Think about how we are related to everyone on the planet. In what ways do our genetic histories reveal connections? What does this mean for addressing global concerns?

We started with spinning a globe and imagining what "there" is like. Now google the place on the globe where your finger landed. It would be great to go there, but time and money likely will not permit this. Instead, work as a small group investigating the first page of websites that show up. Think, talk, discuss, and derive some insight into "there."

Begin again with a list of more probable travel possibilities. From your home, where have you visited by foot, bike, car, bus, train, or plane? Within these distances, what new experiences might lead to gaining insight into how other people live?

Think about other schools, playgrounds, stores of all kinds, occupations, houses of worship, and every other category of people living together that you can come up with. What is interesting? Plan a way of visiting people who live there and engaging in some common interest together. Maybe they have something to teach. Maybe they would appreciate some help. Maybe a plan can be made to share common experiences. Ensure that whatever is planned, there is a good chance the visit will be a lot of fun and maybe lead to making some new friends.

Now, again, stretch your imagination. Might you be able to go further than ever before by gathering new resources and earning money that could make an actual trip possible? Think about a plan where you offer to help out by working together with a group of people you have never met. What would you hope to learn from this trip? Realize that this activity suits adults and young people alike.

Shifting Awareness

It is a given that we need to develop self-understanding and no less that we need to work on imagining how others think and feel. When these two come together, the ability to act ethically is strengthened. Learning about ethics is one thing; acting ethically is another. At any age, doing what we know to be right all too often gives way to doing what mainly serves our own benefits—and all too often caters to our fears.

So far, we have been working on counteracting this tendency by practicing mutual respect in our daily lives. Learning how to truly care about the concerns of others is what counts in developing a well-functioning local community. Now that the focus is on a global level, one can imagine that idealistic tasks are even more difficult. There is an advantage, however. What happens outside our daily lives is emotionally less complicated than what occurs in day-to-day intimacy. Indeed, the unfamiliar, when we get beyond our fears, can be exciting, because it offers endless opportunities for learning. When we leave the familiar behind and allow what is happening elsewhere to inform us, all aspects of our lives can be touched in unique ways. New perspectives unhinge habitual assumptions. It is then possible to gather insights coming from other contexts to refresh those that are connected with our own homes, schools, and towns.

In the global arena we can learn in bold strokes about how others think and feel. On our becoming involved in global concerns, a good measure of empathy can open us to understanding more deeply the connection between our local lives and the world all around us. In books and movies, we read about and see worlds that expand our own. Given the media opportunities of today, there are endless possibilities for learning from this kind of experience. And of course, whatever direct, interactive experience we engage in beyond our daily lives enriches us that much more—be it in another neighborhood or town, a large city, another state, or somewhere else in the world.

Donna's father, Abe, was an immigrant from Russia. He introduced her to a quote from the *Rights of Man* by Thomas Paine: "The World is my country, all mankind are my brethren, and to do good is my religion." She learned at a young age that everyone is responsible for making our world a better place. Human conflicts call on us all to act as equal participants. Abe wanted her to know that getting along with others is practical as well as idealistic. By caring for the health of others we care for ourselves, he would say, because germs don't differentiate between the haves and have-nots. We're all in this together.

When there are opportunities to travel and work with people elsewhere, however close or far away, Westerners must avoid attitudes that reflect a sense of superiority or entitlement over others. There is no place to imagine that our offers of help come from a sense of noblesse oblige or imperialist right—as if a technologically advanced or richer culture has more important knowledge to impart about how people get along. Ethics is about relationship, and relationship is of prime concern for young people. They know they don't know it all. With encouragement, they are attuned to knowing more.

It serves children personally and the world more fully when we understand how similar we all are. Some of this thinking and feeling is easy; some takes a stretch of imagination. Academic discussion about the nature of empathy is less important than engaging in opportunities to explore problems from many vantages. Shifting awareness between self and other is eased by actual changes of perspective. This happens as we move from views of our own community to a community nearby, to communities farther away, to the far reaches of our state, our country, and then other countries. Maybe, too, we gain from stretching our imaginations to the possibility of other universes.

Clipping Newspapers

News comes in many forms these days. Growing up, we relied on newspapers and the radio. For the time being, newspapers are still a

---

Text Box 7.1 Writing a Short Story

The Challenge to Care in Schools by Nel Noddings (2005)

As an example for students, Jerry wrote this short story and made an assignment:

> I hate having all my molecules digitized. Who am I when my existence is nothing but bits on the hard drive? Reassembled, I step off the transporter onto a planet I've never been to before. I know the first question the ambassador will ask me: Who are you? And I want to ask, How do you care for each other? How do you manage your social order?

Rewrite the story, continue it, or write your own. Be sure to include two sentences that reflect ethical concerns. Whatever you do, make the story no more than twice the length of the example. Take your time. Writing a really short story sometimes takes more time than writing one that is longer. Feel the feeling of the story and make sure you like it, for starters.

* * *

"Morality is affected by fear, but it is inspired by love.... Therefore [it is] essential that children be cared for and that they recognize and respond to care. With relations of trust and care well established, they may be prepared to care in the wider world of casual acquaintances, strangers and aliens" (110).

---

common form of media and serve as an evocative tool for teaching. Children can easily work together cutting out articles from yesterday's news. We can also find newspapers online. "Clipping" them simply requires copying and printing out what draws our attention or, better yet, our fascination. On this note, there are probably English-language papers in every major city in the world. Paper or digital copies can yield a rich database.

News reported for the most part reflects conflicts of values. The front section of the paper covers a wide spread of stories that go beyond what is happening in the local community. And local reports sometimes reflect global issues. There is plenty of material from which to choose. There is much to attract a variety of interests.

The clippings can be used to stimulate discussions that relate children's lives to people all over the world. With their clipping mates, they can create piles based on geography, content, conflict, and thoughts and feelings about their interests. Choosing one story to summarize can lead to sharing stories with others and thinking together about how people don't and do manage to get along everywhere in the world. A group of stories reveals the underlying mess that surrounds the more orderly way we try to live. With a little luck, there will be examples of conflict resolution that generate useful learning.

The dark side and the goodness of human behavior are exposed, as are the stories of life in between—bounded by what is deemed newsworthy. Plus, the stories are viewed through the eyes of young people and their curiosity. This is the time and place for a teacher to introduce a list of provocative questions. For example, given their age, is there something too dark to talk about, a topic inappropriate for discussion? What connects with their life experience so much that it seems particularly relevant to dig into? Are there interests connected with opportunities to serve the needs of others they are reading about? Is there work the children could join that would be practical and fun?

Communal Work

Clipping newspapers is just one activity that leads to global thinking. Doing communal work together, locally or globally, is usually experienced as exciting. Accomplishing work and feeling some level of success, in camaraderie with others who are similar in age, is the key. This is the way to help young people grow ethically. The challenge is to begin by attaching this growth to practical experiences. There are always options. Young people can be guided in creating or attaching themselves to projects where the work is meaningful, useful, and enjoyable—particularly because it is done as teamwork. The challenge is for young people and adults to work together, choosing a project that is likely to achieve most of its goals. For this to happen, everyone involved needs to have a stake in the process.

Children becoming adolescents are at an important stage of development. They are seriously struggling with their identities, which are new and often quite different from how they have behaved as younger children. Cultural expectations are changing, and so are those stemming from new kinds of thoughts and feelings. Tensions can pop up at home, with their extended families, with friends, in school, on the playground, and in the community. Viewed positively, everything about their being is striving to expand. They are likely to be reaching out beyond their homes, schools, and communities, and much of this is simply geographic. Branching out ethically is not typical, but encouraging these young people to think about global concerns fits the bill. Even more, this time is ripe for learning ethics.

The feelings of the emerging adolescent start to conflict as their bodies change and their minds grow to incorporate more complex possibilities for relationships. It can be both frightening and humorous for their adults to watch them cycle from absolute knowledge of what is right to very childlike need for adult protection and assurance. As adults, we need to remember our own transition into adolescence and the pain we experienced; it will help us better serve as guides on this journey.

We will remember how important it is for them—as it was for us—to expand the spaces and places in which they live. As guides we can help them find meaningful ways to expand that are not only adventurous but also safe. When young people travel to new places, near or far, to be helpful and make life better for others, they get not only an adventure but a sense of satisfaction and worthiness. The distance is not the issue; the unexplored environment—something different and challenging—matters. Negotiating the unknown is the universal challenge of this developmental process. The job of the adult is to guide while keeping a distance. And it is not science; it is a fine art.

There is important ethical learning to be had by moving some life space out of the home, school, or community. Are there resources that would enable young people to travel, near or far, to realize these interests in some tangible form? Could some or all of these resources be earned? For a school project, do one or more teachers have the knowledge, experience, and contacts to lead a trip away from home or even out of the state? In the family, are there adventures to do together or ways to encourage young people to do them on their own? No matter how few monetary resources are available, there might be ways.

It was wondrous to us how two teachers at the Project Learn School, Jason Huber and Liam Gallagher, had the courage, creativity, and smarts to initiate a trip to Costa Rica for the eighth graders as part of their graduation activities. The students worked hard to raise the money needed for the trip. The learning and the memories are impressive.

A Final Note

Actions taken to address local and global concerns define an ethical stance. But they are not necessarily conflict-free. The creative

Join the ADVENTURE.

Learn from

within, experience & work.

Live with a Costa Rican family, work with a local community.

They'll teach you more than you can imagine...

Support the P.L.S. 8th Grade Service Trip to Costa Rica, Spring 2013

Photo 7.1 Raising Money

confrontation of such conflicts enriches the development of maturity. There is the possibility that one person's actions will contradict the ethical stance of other people. Too often, adults bring to the table no better skills than the children becoming adolescents.

In this meeting ground, everyone stands to become more mature—ethically, compassionately, and responsibly. In a small way, but significantly, high school teachers in Philadelphia often recognize those students who have come from the Project Learn School. They find that our students know how to talk with adults. They don't mean the ability to chat; they are referring to the fact that these young people know how to move differences of opinion toward agreement. This is a skill that too many politicians have forgotten or never learned.

To guide well, we must model. Acting ethically is foremost in the process. The attention to global concerns is a worthy field for doing this work. The age is right, the developmental tasks are on target, and doing projects collaboratively is optimal. Learning to talk with strangers and one another is the elemental goal. This is the beginning and end of learning how to get along with others—the essence of ethics.

Text Box 7.2 Where in the World Do Ethical Principles Come From?

The Power of Religion in the Public Sphere edited by Eduardo Mendieta and Jonathan VanAntwerpen (2011)

Philosophers commonly assume democracies require a significant level of separation of church and state. But Charles Taylor, a highly regarded philosopher among them, differs in a discussion with Jürgen Habermas, Judith Butler, and Cornel West that is chronicled in this book. He argues that the concept of the secular must include the habits of religious thought. Reason and logic have been the prominent domain of secularism. It must be expanded to include other forms of thinking so as to embrace, not exclude, the assumptions that are characteristic of religion. The goal is to achieve a "workable civility" among the world cultures.

> In many Western countries, where secularism initially emerged as a vehicle for protecting against some form or other of religious domination, there has subsequently been a shift toward a more widespread diversity of basic beliefs—religious, nonreligious, and areligious. In these contexts, as others, Taylor argues, there is a need to balance freedom of conscience and equality of respect. (7)

Consider your ethical principles. Which are religious teachings? Which are secular? Which did family and other friends teach you? Which derive from your own mind and heart? What does the concept of a workable civility mean to you? Teaching about global concerns begs for an understanding of these questions and having at least a few answers.

SECTION THREE

TEACHING

INTRODUCTION TO
SECTION THREE

There are different kinds of teaching. They are various means to the same purposes and, with planning, paths to achieve special goals. Varying how we teach is a way to maintain interest in learning. The human brain thrives on variation in general, and this approach to teaching also makes it possible to match up with differences in learning style.

There are times when didactic lecturing is the best way to introduce and organize new concepts and ideas. As important as lecturing is for achieving these goals, small groups serve a unique purpose. Small-group work demonstrates that a teacher is interested in hearing about what the students are thinking and allows for the children to hear each other's thoughts. We should trust that students can use this opportunity to come up with their own, equally worthy ideas. Extending this assumption, we can experience how opportunities for children to teach each other can satisfy the same goal plus enhance self-confidence and self-assurance. Giving students intellectual responsibilities helps them to believe in the seriousness of their endeavors. Topics become more important, and so does how the children think of themselves.

The first of the three last chapters focuses on a teacher's difficulties in the face of uncertainty. Teaching ethics is accompanied by the difficulties intrinsic to the topic. A clarity of leadership is always a requisite for an educative learning environment. Integrating uncertainty into teaching and learning is essential for doing the job competently. It doesn't work to simply smooth out uncertainty; rather, it is necessary to show how uncertainty is a normal aspect of life's work that does not have to undermine good teaching or ethical behavior. The message is to convey that children and adults are both capable of high-functioning behavior—most often as a result of satisfying choices. With this, we can model confidence for our students and thereby teach it to them.

Topics covered in Chapter 8 include the problem of expected tensions that teachers face and a paradox that cannot be resolved. We then turn to two illustrative examples. The first centers on the biblical commandment "Thou Shalt Not Kill" and the second on the existence of evil, which confronts us all at some time or another. The big picture in this chapter is presented as an interaction of the teacher's skills and the monumental problems of the content that must be included in the picture.

Next, Chapter 9 brings in the possibilities that emerge from challenging students to teach other students. We begin with peers teaching each other as a component of small-group discussions. From their reading, students are expected to plan short lessons that address topics they choose. With this experience in hand, they are assigned to teach a student or two from a class of younger children. The texts they use are from a lower grade level—those with more pictures and authored with younger children in mind. In addition, special attention is paid to preparing them with a lesson on listening skills. We, too, have to pay attention to this lesson and model good listening behavior.

In this chapter, we consider ten books that have been unusually helpful to teaching ethics to young people. Using these examples, we can see how John Wall's concepts from *Ethics in Light of Childhood* (2010) have practical meaning. To expect a child to teach another child, we can depend upon youngsters' natural abilities to be creative, to have innate interest in stories to tell and be told, and often to express responsiveness that matches or betters that of adults. Being creative is a trait that puts young and old on a somewhat level playing field. Expanding our narratives is also something we share in common. It is a time, too, for children to learn more about recognizing their obligations to others. The meaning of responsiveness is expanded, leading to behavior that is truly ethical in its understanding. In decidedly nontheoretical terms, the popular success of the books we have chosen can be thought of as evidence that our adult conceptual understanding is on the right path.

For Chapter 10, the finale, the two of us joined with other teachers, mainly artists, and the children to transform the semester's work and end-of-semester art projects into a public ethics exhibit that was hung in two local coffee shops for nearly a month. It turned out to be a grand celebration documented and catalogued in this last chapter.

Asking students to transform their learning into public media was a big step forward. Going public heightened their confidence and assurance in what was learned. Adult enthusiasm and the curiosity of other children about the exhibit translated into students' enthusiasm and pride, whereas before there had been some skepticism about the project. The normal pressure to grade students' work gave way completely to teachers' critiques, which led to improving the work before the show was hung. The "real world" often touted as the grail to which students must answer became the final judge. The daily audiences that came and went gave their seal of approval—often by contributing to a community bulletin board that offered everyone space to post a brief personal definition of ethics.

We ourselves experienced many kinds of teaching with all those who assisted us. Add to this all of the students when they were engaged in teaching children from a younger class. The range of creativity gave the course a special kind of sparkle that enlivened teachers and students. Our many stories about what it means to think and act ethically palpably expanded within us, and our community became more understanding of each other. We grew indeed to understand better our obligations to each other. We didn't so much change our beings as shift the working and playing relationships that made up the junior high community. It was nothing really grandiose, but it was enough to know that if there was a spot of evidence of bullying, every child and young adult knew something had to be said—maybe nothing more than "That's not ethical," as one of the students said to his brother at home one day during the course.

One thing more before we get into the chapters and the details. In retrospect, we noticed how two large exhibits demonstrated well some central principles of the course. Each was constructed out of soundboards, one six by four feet and the other eight by four feet. The first is an unusual triptych hung horizontally, with definitions of ethics written by students and adults. It is intriguing how some of the definitions of the children and the adults are so close you can't tell them apart. A second triptych is traditional, with three side-by-side panels. Each panel is a collage, but all three are closely related to each other. It is wondrous how they were constructed. Eleven students working together introduced samples of their writing and artwork to make one well-connected art piece within each panel and across them.

So we see, the children are fully human, like their teachers, in their ability to define ethics. And their creativity is open to responding to each other to make one piece of art representing many hues. Each has his or her own story that allows for and energizes working together on the meanings of ethics.

CHAPTER 8

YOU ARE THE
ETHICS TEACHER

Everyone reading this book is an ethics teacher. On the job, at home, and everywhere else, we model connected, caring, and concerned behavior—or we do not. We teach young people with our actions and sometimes with our words. We are remiss when we fail to act.

To be responsible, we obviously need to have knowledge about ethics. However, we should not be know-it-alls or imagine that the difference between ethical and unethical is always clear-cut. Good judgment requires an understanding of context. Ethical behavior is best assured when taught with guided conversations among children themselves. No doubt, adults have to impose boundaries, but these boundaries should include the exploration of possibilities. No citizen, parent, or teacher is excused from this work.

The first discussion in this chapter, based on Amanda Berry's book *Tensions in Teaching about Teaching* (2007), concerns an underlying tension between confidence and uncertainty. The meaning of core values is clarified and, with this, how the personal development of these values enhances a sense of confidence (Kim and Greene 2011). Next is the interactive role of knowledge and intuition in the practice of teaching (Allender and Allender 2008; Atkinson and Claxton 2000). Finally, we confront difficult examples. Recognizing how uncertainty, establishing core values, and making room for intuition enter into the curriculum, we offer two plans: one addresses permissible acts of killing, and the other, coping with evil.

Confidence and Uncertainty

Teaching ethics is not easy. Uncertainty is part of the package. The work, in contrast, requires enough thinking, planning, and preparation to be able to act with confidence. The beginning questions center around knowledge about oneself. Particularly as regards the classroom, how do we model the behaviors that we expect of young people? How will we need to change in order to set an example? What core values underlie our self-images? Can they be articulated? What do we want the children to know and demonstrate? Our failings are part of the picture as well. It is disingenuous to pretend that we are more ethical than we are, and it is counterproductive to act holier-than-thou. Knowing this, we are in a position to act with confidence, even with our flaws.

All teachers face classic tensions regularly (Berry 2007). Should we teach students what they need to know or encourage them to learn it on their own? How much challenge can they handle; how safe do they need to feel? When does it make sense to deviate from the plan set forth in the curriculum? How well do our actions reflect our intent? In the teaching of ethics, where does confidence arise in the face of intrinsic uncertainty?

We try to act confidently, but often we will feel uncertain about how to proceed. There are tensions between pushing students too little or too hard, possibly undermining the sufficient comfort that allows us to tap their best learning abilities. Sometimes it is more effective to help children learn on their own so that the knowledge gained is more deeply engrained. These conflicting realities beg for a balance that leads to effective learning—at home and in the classroom. Berry names these three tensions safety and challenge, confidence and uncertainty, and telling and growth. Describe ways you are likely to lean:

Toward confidence or uncertainty?
Toward providing more safety or more challenge?
Toward lecturing or encouraging self-directed learning?

Does anything puzzle you about how you lean? How might you go about balancing these tensions?

To complicate matters, core values themselves can be contradictory and, at times, embrace hypocrisies and ambiguities. Our desire to be honest becomes less certain and difficult when we need to support students who, though they are trying so hard, turn out poorly executed assignments. Another core value can call upon us in this case, at the least, not to tell the whole truth. These qualities are part of our self-development and theirs and need to be explored. A teacher's identity requires paying attention to the hypocrisies and the ambiguities—the path to authenticity is not one that hides the contradictions that are felt and require creative expression.

Strength lies in differences within ourselves, within others, and between us. Out of this reality we have to use our creativity to discover where there is common ground and where there can be change on which to build authentic relationships. Moreover, we are likely to declare some of our values absolute. For these, we need to recognize how they limit the amount of common ground that can emerge; we must also recognize that they are a necessary part of the big picture. We hold as absolute the need to interact openly with others. We strive to encourage intellectual and emotional engagement with young people, strengthening the likelihood that they will abide by expectations set both by adults and by themselves. Other absolute values necessarily concern bodily harm, and such problems in the long run are better handled by discovering common ground—after we do whatever is necessary to stop any harm that is happening immediately.

Teaching ethics is not limited to a person who is in charge of an ethics course. For teachers and nonteachers alike, there are everyday opportunities for teaching. Much of what is taught need not be in response to crisis. Anytime we model ethical behavior or successfully challenge children to act ethically, there is what to discuss. We are engaging a teacher's voice, and we can notice how well it works to build interest and draw people into knowing more. Intuitive knowledge about teaching is as important as what we study about guiding learning. These intuitions are based on how we generally interact and connect with children and adults. We have to understand that learning to teach takes place on many levels—and on more when we are studying ethics.

Talking about ethics can easily build resistance. These interactions are opportunities to gain insight into the informal teaching of ethics. No doubt, teaching ethics to children becoming adolescents is a big challenge. Maybe it is easier to begin with observing how our own ethics are developing in the process of becoming conscious of this work. From this viewpoint, we can become more sensitive to our connections with children. We can learn how to push the boundaries of our learning so that we can hear others better and know better how to draw wisdom from children's own thoughts and experiences.

Text Box 8.1 Core Values

"Aligning Professional and Personal Identities" by Younghee M. Kim and William L. Greene (2011)

Kim and Greene explore the contradictory nature of core qualities and find identity development enhanced by paying attention to hypocrisies, ambiguities, and how well authenticity is sustained.

Which ethical principles are you most sure of?

What makes you so sure?

Are there close friends or family who would disagree?

What core values might children easily understand?

How have your core values changed over the years?

Much of this know-how is embodied in the experiences of our lives. This is certainly true for us as adults. If we believe that it is true as well for children, then we have so much to learn from them. There are level fields of discourse even as we maintain responsibility for setting adequate adult boundaries. In this space, in the engagement of connections that take place in this common ground, intuitive teaching strengths emerge. Ordinary knowledge can be transmitted on many levels, and the spontaneous creation of new knowledge can happen. Most welcome is the knowledge that grows out of collaboration. It is delightful when children and adults create together, not knowing who contributed what in the thinking and doing. It is extraordinary when the children work together without direct help, learning about ethics on their own. This is priceless learning. Though our contribution is essential, it is even better when it is not so noticeable.

Being a Teacher

The embodiment of knowledge, with its intellectual, emotional, and intuitive components, is the aim. The problem of choosing the right course of action has a history rooted in patterns set early in our development. We can unravel how we all hold ambiguity as a part of everyday living. We can focus on striving for authenticity. In this process we modify our identities so as to add the role of ethics teacher, a teacher whose self is expanding and who is helping young people to expand their selves. We model best by continuing to become more aware of ethical responsibilities, including our obligations to others, no matter what subjects we teach. Growing and developing children have their own significant identity issues. Our success is measured by how well young people reflect the development of their own ethical consciousness.

Teaching comes in many forms. Some are quite informal. Much of what we have been discussing is somewhat passive—related to observation, responding to teachable moments, and finding ways, when necessary, to help everyone get along, including ourselves in the mix. Other times, we need to take more charge. Certainly, this is true not just in a classroom. It is always the responsibility of parents to provide structure and boundaries while making space for the growth of independence. Besides entailing worrying about making mistakes, being in charge means planning and strategizing ways to encourage and achieve the goals we have in mind. There are times, too, when adults other than teachers and parents might have opportunities to make a dent. This means watching for moments when our lives intersect with youngsters' and acting proactively when it makes sense. There is risk, but challenge is involved no matter what our role is.

Text Box 8.2 The Paradox of the Teacher Self

Developing a Pedagogy of Teacher Education by John Loughran (2006)
Teacher Self by Jerome S. Allender (2001)

"If understanding paradox in teaching is helpful, then the translation of that knowledge … must surely offer helpful ways of conceptualizing a pedagogy of teacher education" (Loughran 2006, 71).

In his final paper, Paul Dixon, one of Jerry's undergraduate students, describes an exciting experience that happened to him:

> Then, out of nowhere, during the question-and-answer segment of my group's panel discussion, it hit me, BAM!!! At that point, I can't remember the exact words that triggered it, but when I went home I finally figured out what I think this whole semester is about. We needed to read our books in order to realize that we didn't need to read our books. Huh? I know I may sound kind of nonsensical, but there is a lot of logic behind these thoughts. You see, what is really important is for us to find the teacher inside of us. (Allender 2001, 145)

Paul goes on to explain how we can only teach in one way, and that is our own way.

Given this paradox, how is it that the ability to teach can be improved? And there are special ways to teach ethics? How do we assure that these ways of teaching reflect our core values?

In our daily interactions, there can be moments that feel out of joint yet not necessarily like problems. Careful observation alone can change subsequent actions in subtle ways. In turn, children respond by shifting slightly. These moments also offer opportunities to query and challenge the status quo. Everyone can be engaged in a discussion of significant misbehaviors—and the ethical concerns involved. We as teachers can share some of the responsibility. For example, maybe the problem has been festering. Could the damage have been prevented at points along the way before it occurred? Are there people present who were in this position?

Observation, responding to teachable moments, and lecturing are important aspects of teaching. For our goals, there must also be a curriculum to guide active participation. Typically, this is a formal process and results in a document. In any event, the same two questions guide the formation of this curriculum: What do we want children to learn? How do we imagine the learning will best take place? In a classroom, the plan requires hard thinking, useful and attractive materials, strategies for engaging the children, and some written instructions, but not too many. Outside the classroom, thinking has to go on, and in all cases, the work rests on explicit intentions and the probable means for carrying them out. Some form of collaboration, including input from the children, helps considerably.

For us, the aim is to develop a conscious awareness of ethical thinking. Our curriculum includes compelling reading usually found in young adult books and challenging writing assigned in the form of short papers. The focus is on ideas that are likely to grab youngsters' interests, imaginations, and feistiness. The ideas have to be intriguing enough to give the teacher a shot at succeeding with every child. They have to be relevant enough to assure that the children can find some application to their lives (see Loughran 2006).

We know that children demonstrate the success for which we strive through thoughtful behavior—for reasons that are intrinsic and not characterized by avoidance of an adult's displeasure. The ideal is to manage tensions between what children want and do and our ideals. This includes the difference between how we teach and what is learned. The challenge is to discover what is true within contexts that make all actions relative. The children we are teaching are changing all the time, and we have to respond to children in ways that consider this moment in their lives. Paradoxically, though our lives take place in a context, we must direct our actions by following some sense of truth within ourselves, something that makes solid sense to us. We must recognize that we succeed only when they are succeeding. For this, we have to believe that good teaching rests on a teacher's personal strengths and good learning on the personal strengths of each child.

Thou Shalt Not Kill

Teaching a unit on the ethics of killing can begin with one of the Ten Commandments as its central focus: "Thou Shalt Not Kill." Either the fifth or sixth commandment depending on the faith, it is a central philosophical and practical tenet for Jews, Christians, and Muslims. It is universally an issue for all cultures based on faith or civil concerns and has been for millennia. Though this makes the commandment ring true and unambiguous, it would be more accurate if it were followed by a parenthesis: "(except under certain conditions)."

Our hunch is to start off with a long discussion based mostly on thoughts and experiences. The topic might seem too theoretical and not connected with the daily life of young people. However, the adults

---

Text Box 8.3 A Letter for Dylan from Donna

The Humanistic Teacher by Jerome S. Allender and Donna Sclarow Allender (2008)

In *The Humanistic Teacher*, Donna writes a letter to our grandson Dylan, whom we have mentioned before. He was just about to enter kindergarten at the Project Learn School. Donna's hopes for his experience foreshadow our more explicit attention to the teaching of ethics now years later.

> Altogether, your school should be a community of families who learn together and work together for the well-being of all. I hope you are in a place where the people have a high priority on the value of caring and challenge. Not only should your teachers care about you, they should emphasize how important it is to your life to care about your friends, your family, and the whole community of humans on this planet. . . .
>
> I want your education to be messy. When children are trying things out and changing their minds and looking for new ways, it is messy (not always neat). When teachers are planning curricula to capture the liveliness of every child in the class, it is messy. When children are allowed to make mistakes and try again and talk to solve problems, it is messy (and noisy too). And I want you to know that you will clean up at the end of the day, for it is there that you learn to clean up the environment as you live in it. (174–175)

in their lives, their families and friends, have a wide breadth of experience, possibly including a range of occupations that can bring the issue closer to home and make it quite compelling. Children too have a variety of experiences with the ubiquitous existence of killing that is a part of their everyday reading, media, and games. Given all of this, we will begin by asking under what conditions they would consider breaking this commandment.

Halfway through the initial discussion, we will introduce a questionnaire titled, "Thou Shalt Not Kill." The first item of business is to choose one of three points on a scale from never to often, with sometimes in the middle. Then, there are two questions: Under what conditions is it legal to kill? In your opinion, does this make it right? The children will be invited to add other questions of their own.

If necessary, we will raise further questions to encourage interaction. Consider the duties of a soldier. Under what conditions does a soldier need to think about not killing someone—knowing that killing is a legitimate part of the job? What about the duties of police officers? How are they supposed to deal with ambiguity? Where does self-defense fit in? What about penalties for keeping or breaking the law? If there is time, we might explore the historical meaning of the commandment in the three traditions of Abraham. What is known or imagined about these cultures and others? What about ancient cultures that predate the complexities of modern civilization?

"Thou Shalt Not Kill" is a great example of right versus right, because the conflicting values can be so blatantly obvious in everyday thinking. The questions we are asking are fair, because we can expect every child to have his or her own opinions. We call them true questions, because each child's answers are no less worthy than anyone else's, including the adults who are a part of the discussion. Some can be found to bear more weight as the discussion proceeds; this would make for an even more thoughtful discussion. We expect the children to learn more about the meaning of the commandment and gain a deeper understanding of right versus right.

Reading and Writing

With energy derived from interest, engagement, and a sense of direction, it is reasonable to restart the discussion on the basis of some reading and writing. The children will be required to write up a brief

---

Text Box 8.4 Avenging a Murder

The biblical book of Numbers, passage 35:16–21, has this to say about killing another human:

> But if he smote with an instrument of iron, so that he died, he is a murderer; the murderer shall surely be put to death.

The same holds when the weapon is made of stone or wood or when the killing is done without a weapon, just with the hand. In every such instance,

> the avenger of blood shall himself put the murderer to death when he meeteth him.

This seems to refer not to a legal executioner but to someone who feels that he (or she) must avenge the murderer of the victim.

How might this have made sense in biblical times? Why is this a problem in today's world? How might this kind of rule apply to a crime of lesser significance? How can right versus right change over the millennia?

---

summary of the initial discussion to share with each other in a small group. These discussions don't necessarily require adult leadership; this is all to the better. But maybe, we will ask them to share their writing with their parents for more discussion at home.

Another hour will be spent on the Internet. A Google search on "thou shalt not kill" brings up nearly 1 million sites about the commandment. Choosing among them does not have to be a confusing and overwhelming task. A simple structure will allow for creative thinking. Each site is considered a source of data. The instructions are to choose one Google page of sites, open them one at a time, read a few paragraphs at random, and make a few notes. Creatively, consider the lot and mull on some first impressions. Talk informally about your thinking with others. Then, write up what you have learned in a one-page paper directed by three questions: What thoughts intrigue you? What confuses you? What would you like to know more about? If nothing, explain your disinterest.

Once the papers are completed, they will be shared with a partner and then used as the basis of a class discussion. The task is to look for different points of view uncovered in the students' research. This may give rise to some interest in pursuing further research on the issue of killing. With time permitting, small groups can be formed to explore deeper problems and then share their thoughts with the class.

Evil

We want to introduce a book that both of us read recently. Lisa Pack, our sister-in-law and a teacher at Project Learn, recommended to us *Number the Stars* by Lois Lowry, about occupied Denmark during World War II. She regularly assigns it when teaching about the Holocaust. As the novel begins, the Nazis have already taken over the administration of Denmark. Ten-year-old heroine Annemarie is not Jewish; her best friend, Ellen, is. Their preadolescent playfulness is contrasted with the harshness of two grim German soldiers who reprimand them on a street corner for running on their way home from school to the apartment building in which they both live. For the moment, their lives still have a semblance of normality. But soon, a warning secretly passed on interrupts their playfulness. The Nazis are coming to take Ellen and her family away to a concentration camp.

A deception ensues that requires Annemarie to attest that Ellen is her sister. There is more to the tale, all of which is guaranteed to make readers of any age anxious—the story is more real than any factual report could possibly convey. Annemarie's own sister died three years before in an automobile accident. Later on, it is revealed that a Nazi car ran her down while she was trying to escape capture. This sister was a member of the Resistance, and now her compatriots, some of them older friends of Annemarie, are making it possible for Ellen and her family to escape on a small fishing boat to neutral Sweden.

Annemarie plays a key role in undoing a mishap that surely would have ended in the death of everyone involved. Under pressure that should not be placed on a ten-year-old, she is courageous enough, once again, to fool the Nazis. It was no surprise to discover that toward the end of the tale, we were both gently crying.

This is an instance in which lying seems to be ethical. How do we as teachers and parents handle this lesson? How do we help our children determine when it is critical to lie and when it is wrong to lie? These questions do not have black-and-white answers; they require serious discussion among adults and children.

There is much to talk and write about with regard to how the meaning of ethics moves and shifts. More evocative is how one confronts imminent evil and acts morally. Mostly, *Number the Stars* is about the courage exhibited by adults and one child becoming an adolescent. There is a place in the discussion for harkening back in the real life of the children we teach and moving forward in our thinking about

---

Text Box 8.5 Effects on Others

My Grandfather's Blessings by Rachel Remen (2000)
Number the Stars by Lois Lowry (1989)

Rachel Remen writes,

> To recognize your capacity to affect life is to know yourself most intimately and deeply, to recognize your real value and power, independent of any role you have been given to play or expertise you may have acquired. It is possible to strengthen or diminish the life around you in almost any role. There is no role that absolves us of the responsibility to listen, to be mindful that life is all around us, touching us. (2000, 196)

Lois Lowry, in her afterword, tells about a young man, a very real person, and a letter he wrote to his mother the night before he was put to death by the Nazis:

> And I want you all to remember—that you must not dream yourselves back to the times before the war, but the dream for you all, young and old, must be to create an idea of human decency, and not the narrow-minded and prejudiced one. That is the great gift our country hungers for, something every little peasant boy can look forward to, and with pleasure feel he is a part of—something he can work and fight for. (1989, 137)

---

stopping a bully. A young person might have to choose between quickly finding an adult, speaking forcefully, and even using physical force or maybe employing clever stealth. There are always different ways of expressing bravery.

John Dewey, a hundred years ago, understood how teaching is an ethical craft. Parker Palmer, in *The Courage to Teach: Exploring the Inner Landscape of a Teacher's Life* (1998), focused our thinking on heart, fear, community, paradox, and more. Today, Emily Bazelon, in *Sticks and Stones* (2013), alerts us to the life-or-death possibilities that bullying presents. The need for courage and bravery is very real—without a world war to fight. Widening the lens, Alice Ginsberg, in *Embracing Risk in Urban Education* (2012), shows us how we can fulfill our obligation to give children opportunities to blossom in their lives. We need to move beyond the real and metaphoric image of death to a child's education. We owe students and ourselves a liveliness that keeps us safe and opens all children to the power and wonder of learning.

CHAPTER 9

LEARNING ETHICS BY TEACHING ETHICS

The chapter begins with an example of junior high students teaching their peers in their own classroom. With this experience in hand, we move to challenging them to teach students from a younger class. In both cases, the students are prepared with help in planning their lessons. In addition to anticipating what they might want to talk about, we also place emphasis on encouraging the young ones to talk about what they have learned—and to listen attentively. For teachers, we emphasize what it takes to engender and heighten exuberance for both of these tasks.

By the time children are of junior high age, they have enough knowledge to engage younger children in an understanding of ethics. They are able to teach in some situations. They can readily assist in reading, writing, arithmetic, and other subjects with their more advanced skills, and this applies as well to the teaching of ethics. For example, an older child can read and discuss a children's story that has a moral at the end. It is not a difficult task to help a lower-grade child become interested in a book with lots of pictures. Junior high students have status in this situation and have demonstrated to us that they are able to take their responsibility seriously. They are typically kind teachers who increase their own understanding of ethical behavior by acting in the role of teacher. Indeed, children of all ages like playing this role. We work it out so that our students feel like teachers when they are discussing ethics while reading a story to a child from a lower-grade classroom.

Text Box 9.1 Big Kids Teaching Little Kids

Books Discussed in This Chapter

The Book of Three by Lloyd Alexander (1964)
The Black Cauldron by Lloyd Alexander (1965)
The Castle of Llyr by Lloyd Alexander (1966)
Taran Wanderer by Lloyd Alexander (1967)
The High King by Lloyd Alexander (1968)
E Is for Ethics by Ian James Corlett (2009)
Pano the Train by Sharon Holaves (1975)
The Butter Battle Book by Dr. Seuss (1984)
Doctor De Soto by William Steig (1982)
Shrek! by William Steig (1990)

Teaching Peers

First, we ask our students to teach in small groups with their own classmates. *The Book of Three* is assigned. It is the first in a series of five books that comprise *The Chronicles of Prydain* by Lloyd Alexander. For young adults, these exciting stories join together into an epic that covers a world of problems, ethical issues, and obstacles. Because the characters are greatly varied, each child understands the tale in a unique way. Over several weeks, we divide up into pairs, then into groups of four, and then into larger small groups as we structure mini-lessons for students to share their perspectives with each other. By identifying with characters that match their personalities, they have much to learn about themselves.

Many years ago, when Lloyd Alexander was very much alive, some of Donna's students had the opportunity to meet and talk with him. One wonderful time, a student challenged Lloyd about the age of Prince Gwydion, arguing that the character was much younger than the author said. After a slightly warm conversation, Lloyd allowed that maybe he was wrong.

The Book of Three, The Black Cauldron, The Castle of Llyr, Taran Wanderer, and *The High King* are loosely based on Welsh myth. On the very first page of the very first book, we find Taran forging horseshoes while grumbling that he should be allowed to make a sword. Worse yet, there are no horses on this farm. It doesn't help either that his importance rests on his job as an assistant pig keeper, a role that stays with him through all of his adventures. In this first short chapter, he also burns his fingers on *The Book of Three*, which he is not supposed to open, learns about the Horned King, who promises death wherever he appears, and, while trying to catch Hen Wen, the oracular pig, finds himself in a dark and threatening forest he is forbidden to enter.

In the course of the grander story, he grows from the age of our students to the beginning of manhood. Through his adventures, he finds, discovers, and creates his identity. His friend Eilonwy, a princess, grows to womanhood directed by a different quest—one that presents pressures to learn how to act in ways appropriate to the royal roles she will assume later in life. In their adventures, together and separately, they constantly confront ethical obstacles and choices. All of this is set in a world where the characters become people we dearly care about and who sometimes die.

Readers young and old have grown to love these people whose adventures heighten with battles in the forests, in castles, and within their own minds and hearts. The tale of Prydain is about trustworthy companions, a few betrayals, and a fair share of poignant achievements. There are good people who set stellar examples, some evil characters you yourself wish to kill, and others who are struggling with what path to follow. We have asked students to read all or some of these books for many years now.

Originally, we read them to our children, later they formed part of the junior high study of literature, and for a while we assigned *Taran Wanderer* to teachers in training. They proved wonderful books in widely different contexts. We have now turned the focus to the study of ethics. Besides *The Book of Three*, another book may come up in the course, as we'll see. Often, once having read *The Book of Three*, children take on the whole of the *Chronicles* on their own with a passion. In an author's note, Lloyd Alexander concludes, "To this extent, we are all Assistant Pig-Keepers at heart."

Teaching Younger Students

An abundance of books for younger children can easily yield an ethics discussion. *The Butter Battle Book* by Dr. Seuss is a classic. Zooks on one side of a wall eat their bread with the butter side down, and on the other side of this wall that divides them, Yooks eat their bread with the butter side up. Over time, a battle ensues with weapons of escalating ability to do damage. The wall grows higher. In the end, two men, one a Zook and the other a Yook, stand on top of the wall—ready to blow all the Zooks and Yooks to smithereens. On the last page, the grandson of one of the men pictured asks with concern, "Who's going to drop it?" Between their thumb and a finger, each is holding a bomb the size of a plum. Our grandson Dylan, ten already, still asks on occasion for his nana to read this story aloud.

There are truly oddball books like *Shrek!*, which features a character now famous probably all over the world. Extra oddball is that the character in the story, written by William Steig, is unlike the sometimes charming and sensitive creature portrayed in the movies. In the original, delightfully illustrated story, Shrek is a bully. His bad behavior is softened in the telling, but when we look at the story closely, the picture of him is all the more offensive because his behavior is supposed to be okay. Still, it's a fun story. And besides, Hollywood has rehabilitated him. Discussing Shrek is all the more insightful when these facets are brought to light and, better yet, when junior high students manage to see them mostly on their own. Is this story a good choice for junior high students to teach kids in first grade? Every teacher must decide on her or his own. Of course, many or all of these young ones might have had it read to them already.

One of the best stories dealing with competing ethical pressures is *Doctor De Soto*, also by William Steig, in which the author fully redeems himself. This bad boy storyteller weaves a beautifully compelling tale that explores the subtleties of right versus right with Technicolor pictures, thoughtful dialogue, and a surprise ending.

Doctor De Soto is in a pickle. Because he is a mouse and a dentist, he has a sign hanging outside his office that reads, "Cats & Other Dangerous Animals Not Accepted for Treatment." One day, under the sign, a well-dressed fox waits in abject pain. As a dentist, Doctor De Soto is committed to doing what he can for the suffering, but realistically, as a mouse, he must protect himself and his assistant, his wife, from harm. When looking at William Steig's illustrations, children can tell they are dear, caring people—um, mice! And we know they are struggling with their morals. For sure, young children identify with their safety concerns as well as the need to help another animal who is suffering. Delightfully, the fox is ministered to with technical skill but also with a stealth that protects the doctor and his wife from harm. They are not only dear and caring, but they are brave and smart. There is a lot to talk about.

A Plan

In our view, *Doctor De Soto* is a remarkable book for older children to use to teach younger children ethical concepts. This delightfully illustrated text raises many fundamental ethical concepts. The struggle that Doctor and Mrs. De Soto face at the beginning of the book is a great example of right versus right. The fox is dangerous, and yet they are fundamentally committed to healing animals in need of dental care.

We suggest the following plan for teachers introducing older children to reading aloud to and teaching younger students. After the older children read the book to themselves, ask them to list the ethical issues they have found in the story. Discuss their lists; ask how the big kids might help the little ones identify the issues while listening to the story. Together, make a list of questions to ask after the story has been read.

These older children should act out the beginning of the book where Doctor and Mrs. De Soto decide to care for the ailing fox. Encourage them to add more dialogue than appears in the text and to be explicit about the conflicts that the De Sotos are feeling: the fear of being eaten, the dedication to healing, the risk of helping a fox, the breaking of their clear boundaries about not serving dangerous animals.

Use the skit as an introduction to the book before the student-teachers read it to the younger children. Have the older students engage the younger child or children with whom they are working in a discussion of the story. They can use the questions generated by the whole group if they choose. They can then make a list with their students of the ethical issues the young ones discovered in this story. After hearing the story, the older and younger children might enjoy getting together in a large group and acting out the entire book.

We were further challenged to think afresh and creatively about our teaching with the appearance of *E Is for Ethics*, a new book for us. Written by Ian James Corlett, it targets primarily parents of younger children but is not without merit for children in junior high. It includes twenty-six very short stories to be read aloud, with a few questions to ask at the end of each. The subtitle, *How to Talk to Kids about Morals, Values, and What Matters Most*, reveals the breadth of topics covered, beginning with honesty and ending with respect. What caught our eye was how the book lying out on our dining room table captured Dylan's attention. Without our asking him, he read a chapter or two every week for many weeks in a row—with a little help from Jerry, who left it on top of a pile of other ethics books that we were look-ing at. Our current idea is to first have junior high students read the book and choose a form of ethics they are interested in teaching to younger children.

The breadth of ethical topics is appealing to us and might com-pensate for stories that are clearly less compelling. Some overlap the broader concepts we use to build an overall understanding. Respon-sibility, understanding, empathy, perseverance, effort, and citizenship are good examples. Forgiveness, courage, tact, politeness, loyalty, and gratitude haven't received so much attention from us. Others like truth-fulness, fairness, helpfulness, and trust might draw younger children and older ones alike because they are typical of their daily concerns.

Till the appearance of *E Is for Ethics*, a grand list seemed too confusing, but it makes sense in the context of choosing a topic interesting and relevant to children of different ages. This broader approach for junior high will be useful for examining more facets of the concept of ethics. When this approach is used with younger children, the work assigned to each child would be limited to hear-ing only one of the stories and thinking about it in a discussion with a fellow student as a teacher. And the experience of this mentoring can happen more than once. Sometimes it can involve choosing from many kinds of ethics or a selection of exciting stories, and sometimes it might focus on one story for everyone to read, like *Doctor De Soto*, that can lead to a discussion that includes younger and older children, as well as adults.

Photo 9.1 Learning Ethics by Teaching Ethics

Text Box 9.2 Donna Looking Back over the Years

It was my joy to have established the Project Learn School with my friends and colleagues, Fran Fox and Nancy Bailey. I asked Fran to reflect on her experience having the junior high students come into her kindergarten and first-grade class to work with younger children.

In my thirty-five years of teaching with Donna, I found it critical to establish in my classroom a vocabulary that made everyone feel safe. When we say to children, "That is your *responsibility*," "You are so *helpful*," "I am so *grateful* for ____," "What a *thoughtful* thing to say," "Divide the treat *fairly*," "This requires that you *listen carefully*," "What a *courageous* thing to do," " I know I can *trust* you to ____," we build a rich experiential base for ethical discussions. By the time children reach junior high, this established language gives students a level of comfort and familiarity with the concept of ethics that can be applied in a variety of situations. Junior high school age students often came into the classroom to read with children, teach and play board games, and work in a multiage group.

When helping these older students plan their reading activities with younger children, I thought it was important to have them use this familiar vocabulary when discussing ethical lessons taught in the stories. Books that deal with obvious ethical questions are good for both the older and younger children. Encouraging students to talk with little children about playground interactions, TV superheroes, and their likes and dislikes about the stories helps to establish a sense of what they believe is ethical.

Listening

More standard books, like those published by Golden Press, are simpler and more familiar to most children. Golden Books, as they are called, have been around for a long time and carry simple messages that are compelling to young children, each in their own way. *Pano the Train* by Sharon Holaves is about a train that loses its beautiful red caboose. As he travels through the countryside, the animals try to tell Pano about his missing caboose as he chugs on by. In the din, all he hears is "You've lost ...," and he thinks they are telling him that he is losing a race. So, he speeds up, making it harder to hear. Meanwhile, the caboose rolls back to the station, which he discovers upon his return. In the end, the narrator tells the reader, "Pano hadn't lost either a race *or* a caboose, but Pano had learned to listen."

How like Pano we all are. Oddly, *E Is for Ethics* does not include a story about listening. We have to look to *Pano* for thinking about its role in ethical behavior. We see listening as the foundation of an ethical conversation. Developing listening skills for talking about ethics began with the junior high students talking among themselves about *The Book of Three*. Now, it is time to apply these listening skills by paying close attention to what the younger children have to say. In this way, the engagement of everyone, older and younger, in the discussion of any or all of the books chosen is better assured. Listening to a story interweaves with the experience having someone older listen in return—to thoughts and feelings about the story.

Planning for Listening

A first-grade teacher, parent, or friend of the family can easily engage children by reading a story to them. This is no less true for older students. But they must be watchful. Usually several stopping points along the way can serve as openers to begin a discussion and explore insights into ethics before the end of the story is reached. And it is intriguing that by playing the role of teacher, the older child is likely to gain more confidence in what he or she knows. Paradoxically, the fullness of this knowledge tends to be less important than the act of initiating a conversation about ethics at their own young age.

For junior high students, the conversation can happen spontaneously, but most times planning is required. Teaching plans can be outlined and discussed. Short papers help in the discovery of stopping points along the way and in an understanding of the kind of ethics built into a story. The lack of a moral example is especially worthy of contemplation in advance. We value the need to allow for spontaneity. But much like jazz musicians, students need to have a framework to follow. "Notes" of all kinds fit better when there is a guiding structure—in learning as in music. The adult role is to guide this preparation and facilitate the discussion of discussion. This is not redundancy. It's good sense.

Teachers can form small groups and push students to make certain that a reasonable amount of preparation does get done. At the same time, they similarly need to allow for freedom of expression of the students' thinking. Each group should share its accomplishments in a large group. While creating an ethical conversation for the junior high, the work models for the junior high students what they might strive for when teaching first graders. Teaching with ease models ease and makes older students' approach to the younger more educative. The adult teacher needs to participate actively but, as much as possible, refrain from bossing. In all its variations, this work prepares junior high students to teach younger children—and we, too, learn about ethics by teaching ethics.

Another aim is to have the teaching experience draw in parents and other adults. Parents can be involved in the planning with their children, helping them exert leadership. Adults in many roles can offer questions that relate to our studies so far—from Chapters 1 through 7 in the book you are reading. We need to help students form questions and to be sure that we don't overdetermine them. So it is with their plan for what and how they will teach.

Ideally, we expect students' plans to reflect a confident understanding of their own knowledge and opinions. The knowledge is built and created on the basis of careful reading and discussion. One task is to find ideas from the readings that students want to highlight. Copying down strong quotes that tell a lot without a lot of words can be very useful. It is on target to relate other stories and other recent learning to their stash of relevant knowledge. The aim is to be well prepared to relate what they know to what their younger students know or want to know. Questions themselves can be introduced that reflect a wider

---

Text Box 9.3 Student-Teacher Reflections

Today in Ethics we read stories to students in Maryanne's group. The stories we read helped us teach them about Ethics. I thought it was a very good activity to do with them. It not only taught them something but me too. They really seemed to appreciate us reading them stories and asking them questions. Although ethics was kind of difficult to teach them, just asking them simple questions about what they thought about some situations in the book taught them a lot. It was still fun for me, and I think that my two younger partners, Zivia and Nilah, thought so too.

Spider pretended to be dead and then ate all the food his family was growing. I think both girls understood the ethical issue in this story. —Irene

I had fun reading to the younger kids, Evan and Jachi. I thought they enjoyed me reading to them, and understood what was going on in the book. They knew the right things to do in the situations that the characters were in.

In one story, the spider didn't do any work, but he wanted the food. Both boys thought the spider should have to work for the food. In the other story, the spider wants to help his mother-in-law plant beans but ends up eating the beans without asking her. Both kids thought this was funny and didn't think he should have taken the beans without asking. —Chris

breadth of concerns: laws, compassion, right versus right, difficult conversations, bullying, community ethics, work ethic, and larger realms, what we have called global concerns.

Caveats

Teaching ethics, whether child to child, adult to child, or adult to adult, deepens and potentially clarifies the meaning of ethics in a particular context. The complexity of ethical problems is brought into the light. Too often, people believe that the most effective way to teach ethics, especially to children, is to boil what they read and talk about down to a pap that unnaturally simplifies the situation. It is as if young people will not see through disembodied black-and-white choices. We cannot hide the reality that children experience in their daily lives. No day goes by in which adults around them and in the news don't display bad behavior. It's not right for adults or children, but imagining that we can make it disappear is both foolish and pointless.

In J. K. Rowling's *Harry Potter and the Goblet of Fire*, Dumbledore, the headmaster of the Hogwarts School of Witchcraft and Wizardry, tells all the students exactly how their classmate Cedric was killed, although he knows that most other adults in the magical world would not want the children to know. He does this because he knows that lying to children is not good for them. "The Ministry of Magic," Dumbledore says, "does not wish me to tell you this. It is possible that some of your parents will be horrified that I have done so.... It is my belief, however, that the truth is generally preferable to lies" (Rowling 2000, 722). We agree with Dumbledore that ultimately we cannot—and should not—hide reality from our children. And we fully recognize that as teachers and parents, we have to struggle with how and what to tell children about hard and perhaps frightening realities.

Certainty obstructs the solution of ethical problems by closing off possibilities. So does believing that seemingly attractive but poor choices will suffice. It is true that we can get used to these choices, but this in no way demonstrates to children that they can realistically realize the opportunities they wish for now and in their lives ahead. It is more fruitful when teaching nurtures connections among people and among ideas and reveals intriguing new possibilities. These possibilities make way for factoring in a fullness of life and liveliness. People who are not caring for each other's needs in a satisfactory manner create problems we are trying to avoid. Success is not guaranteed. Getting more closely connected, though, is the road to compromises that have integrity. Teaching and ethics—and life itself—become an integrated process.

The advantage of older children teaching younger ones lies in the potential of their shared exuberance. We begin with children's books because they can generate excitement. They provoke an understanding that ethics is rarely related to answers. They involve adventures, quests, challenges, moments of despair, and unique endings. This is writing that attracts reading, and the experience of this reading presents opportunities for learning together—through writing, activities, presentations, and then more reading and more discussion. There is much for teachers, other adults, and parents to do to make this all happen. Strong leadership can set the stage to help the young engage in authentic ethical conversations. This sort of learning binds innocence with smarts.

Teachers, parents, and the others who choose to get involved in this approach to learning have to give up thinking that academic achievement is the prime goal. Taking time to engage in an ethical process takes time away from what we think of as the required learning of subjects and academic skills. Taking time away from art, sports, and play is not a healthy substitute. The reward is to have children discovering how to take charge of their own learning, willing to be challenged in whatever they are required to learn, and knowing that any missed aspects of a larger curriculum are within their grasp to learn.

The knowledge is most likely to come to light when adults gently push children in their work. The job of adults is to determine the boundaries within which students can do independent studies. Then we need to back into the shadows as much as possible. Just as we can offer insights, so can they—insights that teach us all on a level playing field. In this educational and ethical environment, the potential is great, and so are the risks. At best, young people will expand their identities; they will learn that they are capable of participating in ethical conversations. They will learn to listen, to offer genuinely thoughtful responses, and to think creatively.

CHAPTER 10

THE ETHICS EXHIBIT

Ethics is especially important for its connection with all kinds of learning. It can be related to most every subject taught: science, social studies, humanities, history, reading, and writing. Ethics is more fully understood if it stands out as the fundamental glue that holds a community together—allowing all other learning to make better sense. To signify this importance, we concluded our ethics course with the creation of an art exhibit. Students, teachers, art teachers, artists, parents, and other members of the community collaborated in making paintings and objects while transforming ideas, definitions of ethics, and essays into a visual presentation that was installed at the High Point and Infusion cafés, two local coffee houses. The ethics exhibit, with the visual enhancing the written, was celebrated twice, with six weeks of community dialogue altogether. The students demonstrated their pride in the hard work they accomplished.

Almost a year before the first spark of the ethics exhibit, incidences of bullying occurred in the junior high at the Project Learn School, which prompted the imposition of an ethics course. Bullying was not foreign in the school, but the incidences were no longer disconnected and isolated. This didn't seem like a sudden outbreak of bullying. Upon reflection, it was more accurately the result of a slow breakdown of the junior high's social fabric. For forty years, since the beginning of Project Learn in 1970, applied theoretical concepts of John Dewey and Carl Rogers, as well as other educators whose ideas were prominent at that time, had seemingly protected the school from such ill behavior. There had always been isolated incidences of one child or two picking on another, but once confronted, such behavior was well and deeply understood by everyone, including the (ir)responsible offenders, to be far out of line. But this time something was giving the offenders a misplaced sense of entitlement. Most telling was the fact that neither other children in the junior high nor the teachers were noticing how the social web was being torn.

Jerry Tells His Story

Since my grandson had entered kindergarten at Project Learn, I had volunteered to assist his teacher and other teachers who teach the younger children in reading, arithmetic, art, story reading, and everything else that came up as needed. For me, it was a fun job. I've taught kids of all ages. Most of the time before retiring, I was teaching students in the College of Education at Temple University. But learning to work with little kids again felt a lot like getting on a bicycle after a long time. I was comfortable and happy, even with having to relearn skills for helping these small students focus on and become engaged in their schoolwork.

Donna, on the other hand, was fully aware of the bullying. As one of the founders of Project Learn, she, too, was active at school. Now retired from teaching and practicing psychotherapy, she was taking time to serve on the administrative committee and assisting in the newspaper and journalism class. In fact, she had some of the junior high kids as students and conversed regularly with the higher-grade teachers.

For a variety of reasons, though, one of the junior high teachers and several parents asked me to step in and help. Some reasons were practical, and some had to do with my teaching skills. Mainly, I imagine the request stemmed from my role in a staff-development course for recently hired teachers. As we worked together, Donna was in a unique position to help me figure out a strategy that was likely to succeed.

Confronting the bullies and victims as the proximal problem seemed inadequate in the face of a need for more system-oriented change. Besides, I had had little experience in more direct approaches to dealing with bullying. It dawned on us that we needed something larger in scope to address the educational environment as a whole. The idea was to work from a more positive position—beginning with the assumption that there would be no more bullying as of that moment. Long experience brings workable authority. It doesn't solve the problem, but it does make room for education that is more positive than using punishment to deal directly with inappropriate behavior. Trained as an educational philosopher and in the psychology of teaching, I decided that teaching a course in ethics would fit the bill. Plus, I particularly liked the challenge.

I'd never taught an ethics course before, and it was a long time since I had taught junior high students. From long experience, Donna likes to say that children this age provide two distinct and opposing possibilities for a teacher: they will bring you to your knees or become the best students you will ever encounter. True or not, I kept the advice close at hand in the planning. Together, Donna and I generated some intriguing ideas that helped to build my confidence. I also had some luck. As discussed earlier, the first time I met with the students a week before the course officially began, I noticed the weekly planners with words about achievement on the back cover and words like "fairness," "honesty," "tolerance," and "citizenship" on the front. I asked each student to discuss the covers with one classmate. Which cover defined ethics? Since every pair easily got the answer right, we were off to a good start. We didn't need to define ethics: they could already use this vocabulary word in a sentence.

An Ethics Course

Another good start had already occurred the previous year. I was having lunch with Ralph, a retired Episcopal priest visiting from Maine, and his son, Eric Moore, who is Dylan's father and my son-in-law. Ralph talked about his experiences teaching ethics to high school students. He told us about the Institute of Global Ethics located in Maine and the resources it provided him for teaching his courses. He talked about some of the lessons he had taught and about the students' and his own experiences that had made the courses exciting and successful. I thought to myself that this was something I would like to do someday. I was already looking for an opportunity.

On Ralph's suggestion, I read *Moral Courage* and *How Good People Make Tough Choices* by Rushworth Kidder, founder of the institute. This was fortuitous but not really lucky. I think teachers should always be preparing themselves for opportunities that might arise. I will agree that my timing was good. Important ideas were in mind. The task was to choose from among them and to create a doable plan of action. I knew that what would unfold would not always follow the plan, but there had to be a structure that could be counted on. Then we could veer from it when useful opportunities arose.

Arranging the Curriculum

Laws were the obvious formal starting point. Civil or religious, they are the figural examples of ethics that will come to mind. In school, the other big item was rules. We tagged them with the concept of majority rules. Students well know these are the common guides to everyday behavior. Young people often feel that they are essentially laws, but in our minds they are less absolute—at least, they generally should be. This view leaves open for understanding the meaning and need for special rules identified as minority concerns. The aim was to stimulate a wider discussion of what ethical behavior involves in everyday life. Finally, with regard to these laws, rules, and concerns, we worried about whether young people are treated, and expected to treat others, with compassion. As to these children certainly, bullying reflected a lack of compassion. The expression of compassion is an important element in an ethics curriculum. Laws, majority rules, minority concerns, and compassion formed the foundation of the course.

Now planning in earnest, we drew up from memory attractive concepts that we needed to include in the curriculum. Right versus wrong is important, but not nearly as intriguing as right versus right. Behaving ethically is more than following the rules, and junior high students are well aware of this—it is what drives them to be their best. It also drives them to challenge their teachers. Discussions that have this larger picture in mind show an understanding of how confronting dilemmas entails a higher level of thinking and feeling than required for just cooperative behavior. Often the latter means no more than "good behavior," which can be translated into following the rules. Some of this is needed too. Dilemmas, on the other hand, require complex human social conversation. Together, these four concepts—right versus wrong, right versus right, dilemmas, and complex conversation—formed the basis of what we thought would stimulate unusual questions and challenging answers to take us beyond a more typical notion of an ethics curriculum.

Practical applications of ethics were easy to formulate. It was a given that bullying would be a major theme. This symptom can be used to alert adults and children to deeper problems. The questioning and building of community ethics were the processes needed to confront the larger target of the course—the breakdown of a well-functioning social environment. This is what really needed attention. Global concerns, in contrast, were familiar topics at Project Learn. A part of required learning, elective courses, and extracurricular ones, they reflected that school's active interest in socially responsible behavior on a larger scale than often found in a junior high curriculum. These programs met the students' interests and generated excitement among them. We expected this positive element to balance their present figural culpability—the hot water that bullying had put the students in. The feeling that some children are all bad was to be replaced with knowledge of where they deserve respect and appreciation.

The introduction of a fourth theme, work ethic, came from Liam Gallagher, the junior high science and group teacher. He noted his dissatisfaction with the level of attention students were paying to homework—particularly in ethics and sometimes spilling over to other subjects. The three of us were clearly caught in the misplaced belief that this normal behavior could be corrected by nagging and drawing in the pressures of other teachers and parents. Liam's contribution to a larger frame of thinking helped us to see a missing element. The concept of a work ethic can be connected with the need for achievement but is not always, it turns out. Learning ethics means practicing ethics, and everyone doing her or his work is a fundamental piece of what counts toward success in this endeavor. Just as community service is the practical element in learning about global concerns, it has to be a part of learning in the classroom. This thinking adds to our earlier discussion of the Protestant work ethic.

The themes of the course were covered in part systematically and in important parts not. They came together at the end of the first semester. At the beginning of the second semester, we presented this chart:

Laws	Right versus wrong	Bullying
Majority rules	Right versus right	Community ethics
Minority concerns	Dilemmas	Work ethic
Compassion	Conversation	Global concerns

We used the chart to locate and interconnect ideas in discussions. These concepts served as contexts for understanding reading, writing papers, and making art. The chart provided ethics "at-a-glance" that clarified our thinking in a relatively easy way. It helped students to have a ready vocabulary that inspired confidence for thinking and talking about ethics. When we finally got around to knowing there would be an exhibit, the chart found its place in the form of multicolored placards

Photo 10.1

hanging from the ceiling. It became the conceptual foundation of the course hanging above our heads.

Though a real plan for the ethics exhibit was still a couple months off, everything taking place in the course put us closer into position for the exhibit to happen. Books were being read and discussed. Writing assignments were completed and talked about. Artworks were made and shared. Decisions were carried out for inviting the help of the junior high teachers, some parents, and a few visitors who could help enrich the course—including a few children from another small school. We were busy connecting the student community with its larger context. And timely outlines of the course kept up with changes as they unfolded.

Definitions of Ethics

During the first semester, students had been participating in a series of exercises that integrated readings, role-playing, drawing, movement, writing, and discussion. Culminating these workshop-learning experiences was a request to write a short personal definition of ethics. They were thoughtful and insightful. It was a nice turning point in our understanding of ethics—for all of us.

On a Thursday, the ethics definitions were handed in. On the following Saturday, on a whim, Jerry also asked five men who were members of his multicultural men's group to do the same assignment, before the coffee and brunch. These men, including Jerry, have been meeting monthly for twenty years to talk about important topics in their lives. Among these discussions, ethics has been a regular focus, and the request, though pushy, was accepted as a normal thing to do. Oddly, when the definitions were compared, it was not always obvious whether they had been written by an adult or a junior high student.

A small celebration was planned for the following week to celebrate the end of course for the first semester. We decided to put the definitions up on posters with a small paper door covering the names of the authors. The party included teachers, parents, and students. Once again, before refreshments, we grouped in front of the posters and discussed each definition. The task was to come to a consensus about whether each had been written by a child or adult. The group got some of them right but, significantly, not all of them. There was a striking moment when the group came to its decision about Matthew's definition of ethics: "Everything. Rules of how things work. How you resolve things." "Adult" was the clear choice of the group. The paper door was lifted, and Matthew whispered loudly, "Yes!" as he pumped his fist up like a young athlete who has just received all tens from the judges. It was a good moment.

At the end of the following semester, the posters were transformed for the ethics exhibit—for a bigger billing set in the context of the larger community that the Project Learn School served along with a number of other private and public schools. As a part of the exhibit, it was hung as a triptych, but in a uniquely horizontal fashion.

Three construction boards, each seventy-two by sixteen inches, were hooked together—one on top, one in the middle, and one below. The definitions were mounted with the names open to view this time. An explanation of the definitions challenged viewers to distinguish the five adults from the eleven students. Visitors tested their judgment and then checked the legend, where the correct answers were printed.

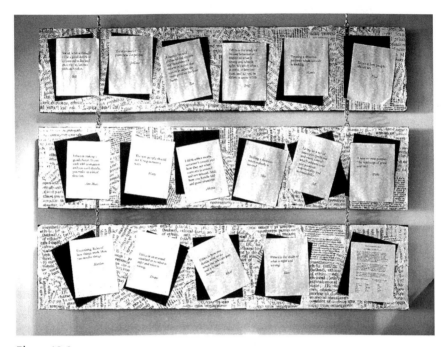

Photo 10.2

The Actual Birth of the Ethics Exhibit

Two more serendipitous events led to creating a public exhibit. One event occurred during the second group meeting of class in the second semester. The other happened at the High Point Café a few weeks later.

From the beginning of class on the first day of the second semester, while brainstorming in small groups, students were making notes with words and pictures using colored pens on three eight-foot lengths of butcher paper. The students were seated and standing around extra-long tables that provided a large enough surface for writing and drawing. The task was to add to the class outline. They were invited to come up with possibilities that would more specifically address their own needs and wants. Finishing up so we could start a class discussion, we prepared to hang the papers horizontally along the walls, but it turned out that the available space was too small. We struggled for a moment and then recognized that a guy-wire stretched along the ceiling would work easily if the three "posters" were hung vertically.

During the discussion, Jerry saw the shape of a triptych normally found in an art museum. The birth of the idea for a vertical triptych was born—to display not this work but three large collages. (This idea also led to the idea of the horizontal triptych.)

The second event took place during a conversation one morning over coffee with Meg Hagele, owner of the High Point Café. The three of us were talking about the ethics course; the conversation led to our wondering aloud whether there would be an interval between the art shows regularly mounted on the walls of the café by local artists. Would it work to hang the work of the Project Learn junior high students some time in the coming spring? The ethics exhibit was going to happen! To begin with, there would be two triptychs on the walls and twelve placards hanging like flags from the ceiling.

The Installation

One wall had more than enough space to hang the two triptychs. There was plenty of room in the in-between areas to put up smaller boards with student papers, interviews, and photographs.

There remained a much narrower back wall to show off the wonderfully evocative photograph of two boys in the "Learning Ethics by Teaching Ethics" lesson: one younger, one older, one short, one tall, one white, one black, one reading, one listening, both deeply engrossed. It's a lovely photo taken by Lucy Miller, one of the teachers who helped

Photo 10.3

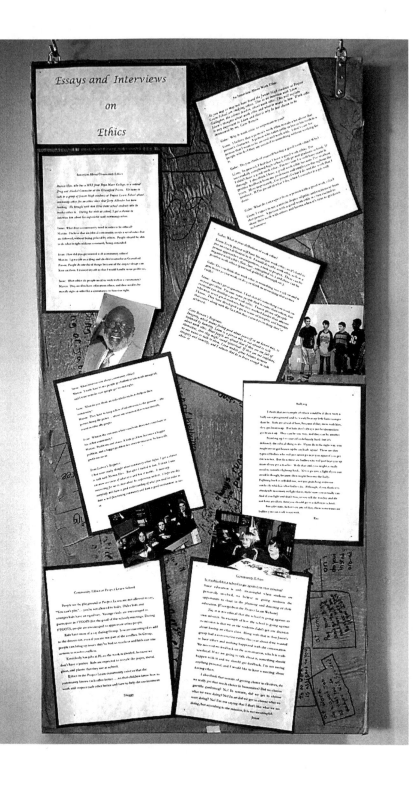

Photos 10.4 (opposite) and 10.5 (above)

plan the lesson. It was easy to believe that the boys' discussion, soon to follow, centered on the ethical problems that unfolded in the story—in kids' terms but more than less poignant.

The wall to the right was mostly taken up with the coffee bar. Between the entrance and where this counter begins, though, the space for tables is doublewide. The wall on the right above these tables was large enough to hang a community board. Donna insisted that we add a board to the exhibit that encouraged baristas, patrons, and children to affix Sticky Notes with their thoughts about ethics. Atop the board was a sign that read, "Share your ideas and definitions of ethics here." The story goes that some of the baristas—who on the

Photo 10.6

night before had seeded the board with their notes for the opening the next morning—insisted that patrons had to affix a Sticky before they were eligible to buy a coffee.

The taking down of the ethics exhibit at the Infusion Café marked an end of the junior high ethics course, but it energized the beginning of this book. It became clear to us that we needed to share with other people who work with children becoming adolescents what we learned from our experience of dealing with an outbreak of bullying. We all care deeply about our students and want them to have the tools they need to develop into responsible, thoughtful, caring adults who are able and willing to struggle with difficult decisions. We hope they will know that sometimes what is right is not so very clear from the onset and that they will have to engage in dialogue and discussion with folks who hold very different ideas and beliefs from their own. And when they are willing and able to spend the time it takes to find the common meaning among those different ideas and beliefs, they will stand on our shoulders and be part of creating a world that is a bit better for their children.

Interested readers can visit the book's website, www.ethicsforchildren .com, for full-color photos and more information about the exhibit.

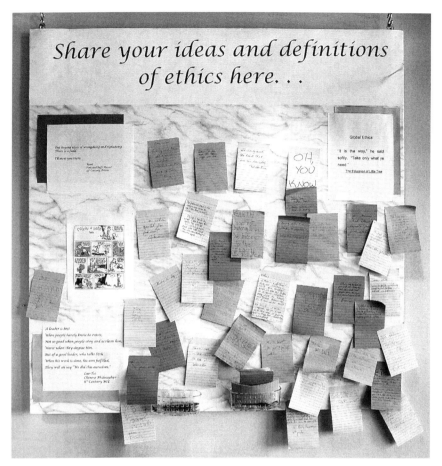

Photo 10.7

REFERENCES

Alexander, L. (1964). *The book of three.* London: Mammoth.

Alexander, L. (1965). *The black cauldron.* New York: Dell Publishing.

Alexander, L. (1966). *The castle of Llyr.* New York: Dell Publishing.

Alexander, L. (1967). *Taran wanderer.* New York: Dell Publishing.

Alexander, L. (1968). *The high king.* New York: Dell Publishing.

Allender, J. S. (2001). *Teacher self: The practice of humanistic education.* Lanham, MD: Rowman & Littlefield.

Allender, J. S., and Allender, D. S. (2001). Gestalt theory for teachers. In J. S. Allender, *Teacher self: The practice of humanistic education* (127–144). Lanham, MD: Rowman & Littlefield.

Allender, J. S., and Allender, D. S. (2008). *The humanistic teacher: First the child, then curriculum.* Boulder, CO: Paradigm Publishers.

Atkinson, T., and Claxton, G. (Eds.). (2000). *The intuitive practitioner: On the value of not always knowing what one is doing.* Buckingham, UK: Open University Press.

Bazelon, E. (2013). *Sticks and stones: Defeating the culture of bullying and rediscovering power of character and empathy.* New York: Random House.

Berkowitz, M. W. (2002). The science of character education. In W. Damon (Ed.), *Bringing in a new era in character education* (43–63). Stanford, CA: Hoover Institution Press.

Berry, A. (2007). *Tensions in teaching about teaching: Understanding practice as a teacher educator.* Dordrecht, Netherlands: Springer.

Blum, L. (1987). Particularity and responsiveness. In J. Kagan and S. Lamb (Eds.), *The emergence of morality in young children* (306–337). Chicago: University of Chicago Press.

Caldwell, E. F. (2000). *Making a home for faith: Nurturing the spiritual life of your children.* Cleveland, OH: Pilgrim Press.

Carter, F. (1976). *The education of Little Tree.* Albuquerque: University of New Mexico Press.

Casson, L. (2001). *Libraries in the ancient world.* New Haven, CT: Yale University Press.

Charney, R. S. (1991). *Teaching children to care: Management in the responsive classroom.* Greenfield, MA: Northeast Foundation for Children.

Coady, C. A. J. (2008). *Messy morality: The challenge of politics.* Oxford, UK: Oxford University Press.

Coloroso, B. (2008). *The bully, the bullied, and the bystander.* New York: HarperCollins.

Corlett, I. J. (2009). *E is for ethics: How to talk to kids about morals, values, and what matters most.* New York: Atria Books.

Damon, W. (1988). *The moral child: Nurturing children's natural moral growth.* New York: Free Press.

Davis, J. C. (2004). *The human story: Our history, from the Stone Age to today.* New York: HarperCollins.

Dewey, J. (1909). *Moral principles in education.* Boston: Houghton Mifflin.

Dewey, J. (1938). *Experience and education.* New York: Macmillan.

Dobson, T. (1983). *Aikido in action.* Tokyo: In Context.

Dr. Seuss. (1984). *The butter battle book.* New York: Random House.

Elbow, P. (1986). *Embracing contraries: Explorations in learning and teaching.* New York: Oxford University Press.

Emde, R. N., Johnson, W. F., and Easterbrooks, M. A. (1987). The do's and don'ts of early moral development: Psychoanalytic tradition and current research. In J. Kagan and S. Lamb (Eds.), *The emergence of morality in young children* (245–276). Chicago: University of Chicago Press.

Etzioni, A. (2002). A communitarian position on character education. In W. Damon (Ed.), *Bringing in a new era in character education* (113–127). Stanford, CA: Hoover Institution Press.

Ginsberg, A. (2012). *Embracing risk in urban education: Curiosity, creativity, and courage in the era of "no excuses" relay race reform.* Lanham, MD: Rowman & Littlefield.

Goodman, J. F., and Lesnick, H. (2001). *The moral stake in education: Contested premises and practices.* New York: Longman.

Henderson, K. (illustrated by J. Ray). (2006). *Lugalbanda: The boy who got caught up in a war.* Cambridge, MA: Candlewick Press.

Holaves, S. (1975). *Pano the train.* Racine, WI: Golden Press.

Horton, M., and Freire, P. (1990). *We make the road by walking: Conversations on education and social change.* Philadelphia: Temple University Press.

Jackson, P. W., Boostrom, R. E., and Hansen, D. T. (1993). *The moral life of schools.* San Francisco: Jossey-Bass.

Kagan, J., and Lamb, S. (Eds.). (1987). *The emergence of morality in young children.* Chicago: University of Chicago Press.

Kegan, R. (1994). *In over our heads: The mental demands of modern life.* Cambridge, MA: Harvard University Press.

Kidder, R. M. (1995). *How good people make tough choices: Resolving the dilemmas of ethical living.* New York: Simon & Schuster.

Kidder, R. M. (2005). *Moral courage.* New York: HarperCollins.

Kim, Y. M., and Greene, W. L. (2011). Aligning professional and personal identities: Applying core reflection in teacher education practice. *Studying Teacher Education* 7 (2), 109–119.

Kramer, S. N. (1981). *History begins at Sumer: Thirty-nine firsts in recorded history* (3rd rev. ed.). Philadelphia: University of Pennsylvania Press.

Kristol, I. (2002). Moral and ethical development in a democratic society. In W. Damon (Ed.), *Bringing in a new era in character education* (173–182). Stanford, CA: Hoover Institution Press.

Kuroyanagi, T. (1981). *Totto-chan: The little girl at the window* (trans. D. Britton). Tokyo: Kodansha.

Levingston, J. K. (2009). *Sowing the seeds of character: The moral education of adolescents in public and private schools.* Westport, CT: Praeger.

Lewis, B. A. (2008). *The teen guide to global action: How to connect with others (near and far) to create social change.* Minneapolis, MN: Free Spirit Publishing.

Lewis, B. A. (2009). *The kid's guide to service projects: Over 500 service ideas for young people who want to make a difference.* Minneapolis, MN: Free Spirit Publishing.

Lichtenberg, P. (1990). *Community and confluence: Undoing the clinch of oppression.* New York: Peter Lang.

Lichtenberg, P., van Beusekom, J., and Gibbons, D. (1997). *Encountering bigotry: Befriending projecting persons in everyday life.* Northvale, NJ: Jason Aronson.

Loughran, J. (2006). *Developing a pedagogy of teacher education: Understanding teaching and learning about teaching.* London: Routledge.

Lowry, L. (1989). *Number the stars.* New York: Dell.

Ludwig, T. (2010). *Confessions of a former bully.* New York: Dragonfly Books.

Mendieta, E., and VanAntwerpen, J. (Eds.). (2011). *The power of religion in the public sphere.* New York: Columbia University Press.

Noddings, N. (2005). *The challenge to care in schools: An alternative approach to education* (2nd ed.). New York: Teachers College Press.

Nucci, L. P. (2001). *Education in the moral domain.* Cambridge, UK: Cambridge University Press.

O'Conner, B. (2007). *How to steal a dog.* New York: Farrar, Straus and Giroux.

Palacio, R. J. (2012). *Wonder.* New York: Alfred A. Knopf.

Palmer, P. J. (1998). *The courage to teach: Exploring the inner landscape of a teacher's life.* San Francisco: Jossey-Bass.

Piaget, J. (1965). *The moral judgment of the child* (trans. M. Gabain). New York: Free Press.

Power, F. C. (2002). Building democratic community: A radical approach to moral education. In W. Damon (Ed.), *Bringing in a new era in character education* (129–148). Stanford, CA: Hoover Institution Press.

Remen, R. N. (2000). *My grandfather's blessings: Stories of strength, refuge, and belonging.* New York: Riverhead Books.

Rigby, K. (2008). *Children and bullying: How parents and educators can reduce bullying at school.* Malden, MA: Blackwell.

Riordan, R. (2005). *The lightning thief.* New York: Disney Hyperion.

Rowling, J. K. (2000). *Harry Potter and the goblet of fire.* New York: Scholastic Press.

Ryan, K., and Bohlin, K. (1999). *Building character in schools: Practical ways to bring moral instruction to life.* San Francisco: Jossey-Bass.

Schultz, K. (2003). *Listening: A framework for teaching across differences.* New York: Teachers College Press.

Shulman, L. S. (2004). *The wisdom of practice: Essays on teaching, learning, and learning to teach.* San Francisco: Jossey-Bass.

Shumaker, D. M., and Heckel, R. V. (2007). *Kids of character: A guide to promoting moral development.* Westport, CT: Praeger.

Simon, K. (2001). *Moral questions in the classroom: How to get kids to think deeply about real life and their schoolwork.* New Haven, CT: Yale University Press.

Spooner, L., and Woodcock, J. (2010). *Teaching children to listen: A practical approach to developing children's listening skills.* London: Continuum.

Steig, W. (1982). *Doctor De Soto.* New York: Scholastic Inc.

Steig, W. (2007; first published in 1990). *Shrek! Plus 5 other stories.* New York: Square Fish.

Sullivan, K. (2000). *The anti-bullying handbook.* Auckland, NZ: Oxford University Press.

Swearer, S. M., Espelage, D. L., and Napolitano, S. A. (2009). *Bullying prevention and intervention: Realistic strategies for schools.* New York: Guilford.

Telingator, K. (2007). Cyber bullying. WBEZ. October 22. www.wbez.org/episode-segments/cyber-bullying.

Tushnet, M. V. (2003). *Slave law in the American South: State v. Mann in history and literature.* Lawrence: University Press of Kansas.

VerSteeg, R. (2000). *Early Mesopotamian law.* Durham, NC: Carolina Academic Press.

Wall, J. (2010). *Ethics in light of childhood.* Washington, DC: Georgetown University Press.

Weber, M. (1930). *The Protestant ethic and the spirit of capitalism* (trans. T. Parsons). Los Angeles: Roxbury Publishing.

Whitehead, J. (1993). *The growth of educational knowledge: Creating your own living educational theories.* Bournemouth, UK: Hyde Publications.

Whitehead, J. (2010). Personal e-mail communication.

INDEX

ABOUT THE AUTHORS

Jerome (Jerry) Allender (University of Chicago, 1962) has been engaged in educational research for over fifty years. His focus is on humanistic education, and most recently he coauthored, with Donna, *The Humanistic Teacher: First the Child, Then Curriculum.* For many years, he was the chairperson of the Psychoeducational Processes Department at Temple University, where he developed the Arts and Science of Teaching course for both undergraduate and graduate students. With his Temple student teachers, he taught children from kindergarten through junior high at Project Learn School. Since his retirement, he has continued to work with Project Learn teachers and students and devotes more time than ever to playing his trumpet at local cafes.

Donna Sclarow Allender, cofounder of the Project Learn School in Philadelphia in 1970 and its Educational Coordinator for many years, has been a teacher for over fifty years. As a member of the American Educational Research Association, her research focuses on the Self-Study of Teacher Education Practices. She is now a practicing psychotherapist working with individuals, couples, adolescents, and groups. Donna and Jerry live in Philadelphia, six blocks from their children and grandson.